T0156134

Lecture Notes of the Institute for Computer Sciences, Social Informatics and Telecommunications Engineering 511

The LNICST series publishes ICST's conferences, symposia and workshops.
   LNICST reports state-of-the-art results in areas related to the scope of the Institute.
   The type of material published includes

- Proceedings (published in time for the respective event)
- Other edited monographs (such as project reports or invited volumes)

   LNICST topics span the following areas:

- General Computer Science
- E-Economy
- E-Medicine
- Knowledge Management
- Multimedia
- Operations, Management and Policy
- Social Informatics
- Systems

Wei Wang · Jun Wu

Editors

Broadband Communications, Networks, and Systems

13th EAI International Conference, BROADNETS 2022
Virtual Event, March 12–13, 2023
Proceedings

Editors
Wei Wang ⓘ
Harbin Engineering University
Harbin, Heilongjiang, China

Jun Wu ⓘ
Shanghai Jiao Tong University
Shanghai, China

ISSN 1867-8211 ISSN 1867-822X (electronic)
Lecture Notes of the Institute for Computer Sciences, Social Informatics
and Telecommunications Engineering
ISBN 978-3-031-40466-5 ISBN 978-3-031-40467-2 (eBook)
https://doi.org/10.1007/978-3-031-40467-2

This Springer imprint is published by the registered company Springer Nature Switzerland AG
The registered company address is: Gewerbestrasse 11, 6330 Cham, Switzerland

Preface

We are delighted to introduce the proceedings of the 2022 European Alliance for Innovation (EAI) 13th EAI International Conference on Broadband Communications, Networks, and Systems (BROADNETS 2022). This conference brought together researchers, developers and practitioners around the world who focus on broadband networks, communication, software, and application systems. The theme of BROADNETS 2022 was "5G-enabled digital society".

BROADNETS 2022 included one main track and one invited track. The technical proceedings published from the BROADNETS 2022 conference consists of 9 papers from a total of 32 submissions, which can be divided into three groups, that is "Mobile Communication Networks", "Mobile Software Security" and "Algorithm, Model and Application".

Coordination with the steering chair, Imrich Chlamtac, was essential for the success of the conference. We sincerely appreciate his constant support and guidance. It was also a great pleasure to work with such an excellent organizing committee team for their hard work in organizing and supporting the conference. In particular, the Technical Program Committee, led by our TPC Co-chairs, Yun Lin, Guowei Shen and Xiaofeng Li completed the peer-review process of technical papers and made a high-quality technical program. We are also grateful to the Conference Managers, Karina Ogandjanian and Mikita Yelnitski, for their support and to all the authors who submitted their papers to the BROADNETS 2022 conference.

We strongly believe that the BROADNETS conference provides a good forum for all researchers, developers and practitioners to discuss all science and technology aspects that are relevant to broadband networks. We also expect that the future BROADNETS conferences will be as successful and stimulating, as indicated by the contributions presented in this volume.

Wei Wang
Jun Wu
Ali Kashif Bashir
Xi (James) Zheng

Organization

Steering Committee

Imrich Chlamtac	University of Trento, Italy
Wei Wang	Harbin Engineering University, China

Organizing Committee

General Chair

Wei Wang	Harbin Engineering University, China

General Co-chair

Jun Wu	Shanghai Jiao Tong University, China

TPC Chair and Co-chair

Ali Kashif Bashir	Manchester Metropolitan University, UK
Xi (James) Zheng	Macquarie University, Australia

Sponsorship and Exhibit Chair

Lanxin Sun	Harbin Engineering University, China

Local Chair

Gang Liu	Harbin Engineering University, China

Workshops Chair

Gang Li	Deakin University, Australia

Publicity and Social Media Chair

Yingjie Wang   Yantai University, China

Publications Chair

Yan Wang   Harbin Engineering University, China

Web Chair

Haowen Tan   Kyushu University, Japan

Posters and PhD Track Chair

Ye Zhu   Deakin University, Australia

Panel Chair

Yun Lin   Harbin Engineering University, China

Demos Chair

Guangxian Li   Guangxi University, China

Tutorial Chairs

Gang Li   Deakin University, Australia
Yingjie Wang   Yantai University, China

Technical Program Committee

Peihan Qi   Xidian University, China
Chi-Hua Chen   Fuzhou University, China
Zhenyu Na   Dalian Maritime University, China
Jinbo Xiong   Fujian Normal University, China
Mingqian Li   Xidian University, China
Zengpeng Li   Shandong University, China
Xi Lin   Shanghai Jiao Tong University, China
Yulei Wu   University of Exeter, UK
Jianwen Xu   Muroran Institute of Technology, Japan

Contents

Mobile Communication Networks

A New Approach for Measuring Delay in 5G Cellular Networks

David Candal-Ventureira⬤, Felipe Gil-Castiñeira⬤,
Francisco Javier González-Castaño$^{(\boxtimes)}$⬤, and Pablo Fondo-Ferreiro⬤

Information Technologies Group, atlanTTic, University of Vigo, Vigo, Spain
{dcandal,xil,javier,pfondo}@gti.uvigo.es

Abstract. 5G networks have introduced new technologies and paradigms to support new use cases with very demanding quality of service (QoS) requirements, in terms of metrics such as delay or reliability. Accordingly, operators need new tools to measure these metrics in different realistic, often extreme, conditions, so that they can evaluate the degree of fulfilment of their service levels. In this work we propose a simple practical framework to evaluate the delay between two nodes in such a cellular network. This framework allows evaluating the delay in the uplink and downlink channels independently. We have validated the proposed framework on top of a real 5G network, by measuring the delay as a function of the requested data rates of the network in different network slices.

Keywords: 5G · Network performance analysis · Network slicing

1 Introduction

Many services requiring wireless connectivity benefit from the advantages of mobile network technologies over other radio access technologies (RATs), such as ubiquity, better performance on the move, and efficient modulation and codification management. However, some quality of service (QoS) requirements of the former are difficult to meet when a large number of users demanding heterogeneous services share the network.

5G standardization is defining architectures, technologies and mechanisms to support use cases that were unfeasible in previous generations of mobile networks. On the one hand, the performance of mobile networks has been significantly improved, with very high transmission rates, very low delays, better

This research has been partially supported by the Spanish grant PRE2021-098290, funded by MCIN/AEI/10.13039/501100011033 and FSE+, PDC2021-121335-C21, PID2020-116329GB-C21 and ED431C 2022/04, and was conducted under the framework of the project "Factory competitiveness and electromobility through innovation", with reference IN854A 2020/01, funded by the agency GAIN from the Xunta de Galicia regional government of Spain.

W. Wang and J. Wu (Eds.): BROADNETS 2023, LNICST 511, pp. 3–12, 2023.
https://doi.org/10.1007/978-3-031-40467-2_1

mobility management and lower power consumption. In addition, the 5G standard introduces the possibility of creating private mobile networks. This allows end users to create their own wireless local area networks (WLANs) using mobile network technology, similarly to Wi-Fi. This kind of architecture requires, however, the operation in shared frequencies, either in industrial, scientific and medical (ISM) bands or bands regulated by governments for specific use cases such as industrial ones. As a result, private mobile networks have significantly less frequency resources than operator networks to operate. In order to support simple devices with limited power and computation resources, the concept of bandwidth parts (BWPs) allows 5G network channels to be divided into sub-channels, in pre-set time periods, so that these devices can be connected to the network by monitoring and transmitting on a short range of frequencies while the rest of the channel is exploited by devices with higher capacities.

A fundamental feature for supporting use cases with special requirements is network slicing. The network slicing paradigm allows the creation of logical networks on a common hardware architecture, which are isolated from each other and have different priority levels. In other words, network slicing allows verticals sharing hardware resources while avoiding mutual interference. This makes possible to guarantee a ratio of the network resources to a certain use case, but at the same time these reserved resources can be assigned to other slices in case they are not being used. Therefore, the network slicing paradigm supports the compliance of a certain level of performance in terms of instant transmission rate, delay, jitter and confidentiality, among other metrics, without network oversizing and allocation of dedicated isolated resources to each vertical, so that the instantaneous demands of one do not affect the others, saving costs for operators. Nevertheless, as different network slices may share a common physical infrastructure, adequate performance measurement systems are essential to operators to meet the requirements they agree with their users.

In this paper we propose a novel framework to evaluate the delay between two nodes within a cellular network. The framework allows to measure the communications delay of the uplink and downlink channels individually. We experimentally validate the proposed framework in a real 5G network setup using commercial end devices.

The rest of the paper is structured as follows. Section 2 discusses related work. Section 3 describes the framework proposed for measuring the delay between two nodes in a 5G network. The setup in which the experiments were conducted is introduced in Sect. 4. Section 5 presents the results of the evaluations. Finally, Sect. 6 concludes the paper.

2   Related Work

Previous analytical works have focused on estimating the theoretical maximum performance supported by the radio interface of a mobile network based on the physical layer characteristics defined in their standards. For example, in [4], the authors analyze the details of the 5G radio interface to compute the maximum theoretical performance it can achieve in terms of peak rate, delay, efficiency and mobility. Similarly, in [7], the authors compare the maximum performance of the radio link for the different 5G radio configurations. In [1], a theoretical analysis of the scalability of a 5G core is presented in terms of CPU load, response time and number of requests per second from different components of the core. This evaluation focuses on the computing resources required to deploy the core rather than on network performance.

There is scarce practical work in the literature evaluating the performance of mobile networks. For example, in [9], the authors evaluate a real commercial LTE network, in particular signal quality parameters perceived by a UE in motion, and compare them to those observed when the UE is static, as well as the throughput in both cases.

Nevertheless, there exist experimental tools and research projects on experiments with mobile networks. Simulation tools such as 5G-LENA [8] and 5G K-SimNet [3] allow estimating the performance of a 5G network by taking into account parameters such as received signal power and interference between base stations. Testbeds such as that of the 5GENESIS project [13] have tested mobile networks using development tools such as software-defined radio (SDR) and open source software.

Network slicing is one of the latest innovations introduced in 5G. As a result, there is plenty of related work in the literature. Most of these articles, however, consider the problem of allocating hardware resources to slices based on demands and QoS requirements [10–12]. In [6], the authors propose a list of specific Key Performance Indicators (KPIs) for network slicing. However, these are intended only for Operations Support Systems (OSSs), for measuring the times to deploy, configure and retire a network slice instance or the efficiency of resource allocation of a slice.

One of the main difficulties when evaluating end-to-end network slicing in a 5G network is the lack of experimentation tools supporting this feature, especially at the Radio Access Network (RAN) side [2]. As a result, there is very little experimental work, mostly led by major cellular network equipment vendors. In [5], a carrier-grade Ericsson 5G testbed supporting network slicing is demonstrated. The authors configure two network slices for Unmanned Aerial Vehicle (UAV) control and data traffic communications, and they demonstrate that control communications in one slice are not affected by the transmissions in the other.

Despite being one of the main concerns of mobile operators, the evaluation of the performance of mobile networks is a field in which there is still considerable work to be done. Certainly, many approaches for evaluating the performance of wired networks or WLANs could be adapted to measure a mobile network, but these networks have particularities that should be accounted for. As previously said, next-generation mobile networks, especially 5G networks, are designed to support services with very diverse requirements and include new paradigms such as network slicing that are relevant to the performance evaluation methodology. Besides, there are substantial differences with previous technologies. For example, cellular transmissions are scheduled, so that end users can perceive different QoS levels. An outstanding difference is the performance asymmetry of the downlink and uplink channels. They usually have widely differing amounts of resources, and, in the uplink transmission, resource grants must be notified in advance to the UE. Therefore, traditional tools to measure network delays, which compute the round-trip time (RTT) delay, are unsuitable for these networks. In this work, we present a framework for separately measuring the delay of any channel/network slice, which is disaggregated by uplink and downlink components. We are not aware of any previous work addressing this practical problem methodically.

3 Evaluation Framework and Methodology

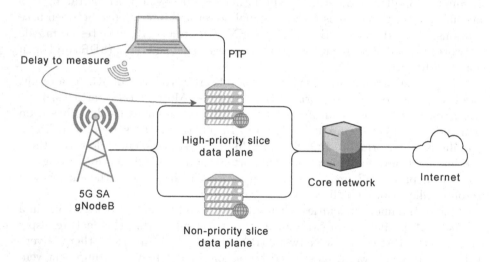

Fig. 1. Architecture of the evaluation framework to measure delays in a cellular network.

Figure 1 shows the framework that is proposed for measuring delays in cellular networks. In this framework, it is necessary to synchronize the clocks of the two nodes between which the delay is being measured. Once they are synchronized with enough precision, the delay can be measured by simply comparing the timestamps at which a series of packets where transmitted and received.

In our evaluations, we have measured the delay in the uplink channel from the UE to the User Plane Function (UPF). The architecture of the measurement testbed is shown in Fig. 1. Both the UE and the server running the UPF were directly connected through an Ethernet cable and ran the Precision Time Protocol (PTP), which has sub-microsecond clock accuracy, to get their clocks synchronized.

Even though perfect synchronization between the corresponding nodes is unfeasible, the deviation between the clocks of the UE and the UPF was three orders of magnitude lower than the values of the delay measurements in our evaluations, which validates the feasibility of our proposal.

In order to facilitate the measurement of the delay, we generated a synthetic packet trace for each scenario under evaluation, by setting the appropriate times-tamps to meet the desired requested data rate. We used the well-known *tcpreplay* tool to send these packets through the 5G network from the UE.

4   Experimental Setup

The 5G Standalone (SA) network testbed that was used for the evaluation conducted in this work is composed of an Open5GS core network and a carrier-grade Release 15 indoor gNB donated by a mobile operator. The network is deployed in our premises, using commercial frequencies temporarily ceded by the operator, which currently does not use them for any service in the area. That is, we were the only users operating on these frequencies in the coverage area of the gNB. Four network slices were implemented and configured in the core network and RAN, covering the most relevant data services.

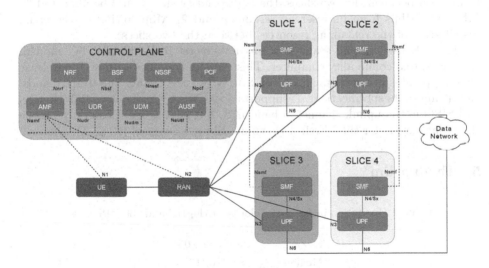

Fig. 2. Architecture of the 5G SA testbed core network.

The 5G core is deployed on an Kubernetes cloud. We isolated the control plane virtual network functions (VNFs) from the data plane VNFs of each slice by deploying them in different machines. A partition like that in Fig. 2 was chosen for its deployment. In this architecture, we have one independent Session Management Function (SMF) and one UPF for each slice, both running on a single host. The control plane host runs the shared Access and Mobility management Function (AMF), the Authentication Server Function (AUSF), the Binding

Support Function (BSF), the Network Repository Function (NRF), the Network Slice Selection Function (NSSF), the Policy Control Function (PCF), and the Unified Data Management (UDM) and Unified Data Repository (UDR) VNFs, which are shared by the four slices. Each host is a server equipped with an Intel Xeon Gold 6230 processor, with 20 cores with a maximum turbo frequency of 3.90 GHz.

The gNB is composed by an indoor carrier-grade Remote Radio Head (RRH) managed by a carrier grade Base Band Unit (BBU). These elements are directly connected through an Ethernet cable. The gNB operates in the n78 band using a bandwidth of 50 MHz with a subcarrier spacing of 30 kHz, and supports 4×4 Multiple-Input Multiple-Output (MIMO). A network switch interconnects the RRU with the data center were the core network is deployed.

The evaluation was conducted in the uplink channel, in which the network was able to provide up to 55 Mbps to Single-Input Single-Output (SISO) UEs. Two networks slices were used, for priority and non-priority services: 20% uplink resources were reserved for the high-priority slice in the RAN, whereas the non-priority slice had no reserved resources. This means that the network guaranteed at least 11 Mbps at the uplink channel. The remaining uplink resources were equally distributed within active network slices until they did not have any pending data to be transmitted. Therefore, in the worst case, when there was contention between the two slices, the high-priority slice would be allocated 33 Mbps (11 Mbps from its reserved resources and 22 Mbps owing to the equal distribution of the remaining resources between the two slices).

The UE used in the evaluation was a Quectel RM500Q-AE[1] 5G modem connected to a commodity computer. This modem complies with 3GPP Release 15 and operates in a wide range of Non-SA (NSA) and SA 5G Sub-6 GHz bands. According to its specifications, it supports 4×4 MIMO in the downlink channel and SISO in the uplink channel in band n78, but in practice it can only handle three data layers for the Physical Downlink Shared Channel (PDSCH) channel.

5   Evaluation

Table 1. Deviation between the clocks of the UE and the UPF (μs).

Mean	4.017e−05
Median	−0.004
Minimum	−9.643
Maximum	10.368
10th percentile	−0.417
90th percentile	0.401
Std. deviation	1.102

---

[1] https://www.quectel.com/product/5g-rm500q-ae.

Before measuring the delay of the transmissions in the 5G network, the deviation between the clocks of the UE and the UPF was computed. If the UPF clock is ahead of the UE clock, the value is positive (and negative otherwise). Table 1 shows the value of this metric during the evaluations. As shown in the table, the deviation between the clocks of the two nodes, once synchronized using PTP through an Ethernet interface, was less than 10 microseconds with an average of 0.04 nanoseconds. These values are far below the lowest delays of a 5G network, which are in the order of few milliseconds. Thus, the error introduced by the synchronization of the devices is negligible.

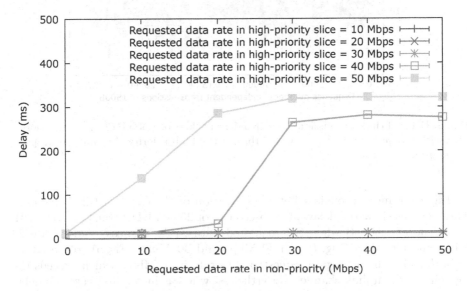

Fig. 3. Delay of the transmission of independent packets of 1,500 B on the high-priority slice versus the requested data rate on slices 1 and 2.

Figure 3 shows the observed delays in milliseconds of the transmissions of independent UDP packets with a payload of 1,500 Bytes in the uplink channel through the high-priority slice between the UE and the corresponding UPF, as a function of the data rate requested by the UE in slices 1 and 2. The figure shows that delay grows very fast when the aggregate requested data rate from both slices is greater than the uplink channel capacity, 55 Mbps, or when the requested data rate in the high-priority slice is higher than 30 Mbps. On the other hand, the average delay stays around 12 ms when the requested data rate in the high-priority slice is 30 Mbps at most, for any requested data rate in the non-priority slice.

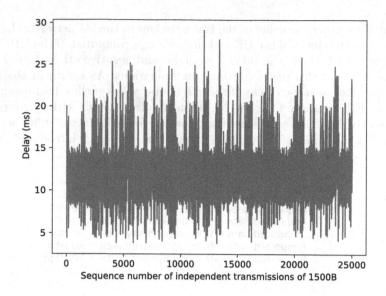

Fig. 4. Delay of the transmission of independent packets of 1,500 B on the high-priority slice with a requested data rate of 20 Mbps in the high-priority slice and 50 Mbps in the non-priority slice.

Figures 4 and 5 provide a better illustration of the cause of this behaviour. These figures show the delay, in milliseconds, of 25,000 UDP transmissions with a payload of 1,500 B when the requested data rates in slices 1 and 2 are 20 Mbps and 50 Mbps (Fig. 4) and 40 Mbps and 30 Mbps (Fig. 5), respectively. In both cases, the aggregate requested data rate is 70 Mbps, which exceeds the capacity of the uplink channel. Nevertheless, whereas in the first case the delay seems constant and has a standard deviation of 3.427 ms around an average of 12.541 ms, it increases gradually in the second, growing from tens of milliseconds to up to 426.541 ms. This is because, as the high-priority slice has 20% of the resources reserved at the RAN while the remaining resources are distributed equally between both slices and the capacity of the uplink channel is 55 Mbps, the high-priority slice receives at least 33 Mbps regardless of the requested data rate in the non-priority slice. When the requested data rate exceeds the resources that are provided to the slice, more and more packets get queued, increasing the delay.

By replicating our setup, any operator or researcher can easily measure the delay KPI of a 5G network to better characterize its operation and ensure that its slices provide the expected quality.

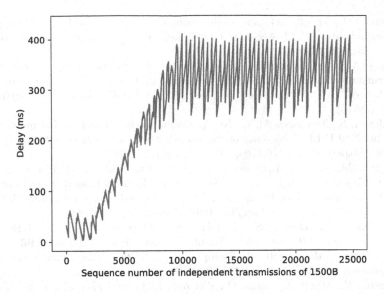

Fig. 5. Delay of the transmission of independent packets of 1,500 B on the high-priority slice with a requested data rate of 40 Mbps in the high-priority slice and 30 Mbps in the non-priority slice.

6   Conclusion

The new stringent use cases that new generation cellular networks seek to support require operators to provide differentiated traffic treatment, highly tailored to customers' needs. Operators should evaluate the compliance of their SLAs under different conditions. In this paper we propose a novel framework to evaluate delay in 5G networks. This framework is specifically suited for cellular networks, as it allows to measure the target metric in the uplink and downlink channels independently. It has been validated in a real 5G network setup using commercial end devices. Evaluation results are consistent with the expected performance of the network.

References

1. Arteaga, C.H.T., Ordoñez, A., Rendon, O.M.C.: Scalability and performance analysis in 5G core network slicing. IEEE Access **8**, 142086–142100 (2020). https://doi.org/10.1109/ACCESS.2020.3013597
2. Chavhan, S., Ramesh, P., Chhabra, R.R.S., Gupta, D., Khanna, A., Rodrigues, J.J.P.C.: Visualization and performance analysis on 5G network slicing for drones. In: DroneCom 2020, pp. 13–19. Association for Computing Machinery, New York (2020). https://doi.org/10.1145/3414045.3416208
3. Choi, S., et al.: 5G K-SimNet: end-to-end performance evaluation of 5G cellular systems. In: 2019 16th IEEE Annual Consumer Communications Networking Conference (CCNC), pp. 1–6 (2019). https://doi.org/10.1109/CCNC.2019.8651686

4. Fuentes, M., et al.: 5G new radio evaluation against IMT-2020 key performance indicators. IEEE Access **8**, 110880–110896 (2020). https://doi.org/10.1109/ACCESS.2020.3001641
5. Garcia, A.E., et al.: Performance evaluation of network slicing for aerial vehicle communications. In: 2019 IEEE International Conference on Communications Workshops (ICC Workshops), pp. 1–6 (2019). https://doi.org/10.1109/ICCW.2019.8756738
6. Kukliński, S., Tomaszewski, L.: Key performance indicators for 5G network slicing. In: 2019 IEEE Conference on Network Softwarization (NetSoft), pp. 464–471 (2019). https://doi.org/10.1109/NETSOFT.2019.8806692
7. Mhedhbi, M., Morcos, M., Galindo-Serrano, A., Elayoubi, S.E.: Performance evaluation of 5G radio configurations for industry 4.0. In: 2019 International Conference on Wireless and Mobile Computing, Networking and Communications (WiMob), pp. 1–6 (2019). https://doi.org/10.1109/WiMOB.2019.8923609
8. Patriciello, N., Lagen, S., Bojovic, B., Giupponi, L.: An E2E simulator for 5G NR networks. Simul. Model. Pract. Theory **96**, 101933 (2019). https://doi.org/10.1016/j.simpat.2019.101933. https://www.sciencedirect.com/science/article/pii/S1569190X19300589
9. Sevindik, V., Wang, J., Bayat, O., Weitzen, J.: Performance evaluation of a real long term evolution (LTE) network. In: 37th Annual IEEE Conference on Local Computer Networks - Workshops, pp. 679–685 (2012). https://doi.org/10.1109/LCNW.2012.6424050
10. Wang, G., Feng, G., Quek, T.Q.S., Qin, S., Wen, R., Tan, W.: Reconfiguration in network slicing-optimizing the profit and performance. IEEE Trans. Netw. Serv. Manag. **16**(2), 591–605 (2019). https://doi.org/10.1109/TNSM.2019.2899609
11. Wang, H., Wu, Y., Min, G., Xu, J., Tang, P.: Data-driven dynamic resource scheduling for network slicing: a deep reinforcement learning approach. Inf. Sci. **498**, 106–116 (2019). https://doi.org/10.1016/j.ins.2019.05.012. https://www.sciencedirect.com/science/article/pii/S0020025519303986
12. Xu, Q., Wang, J., Wu, K.: Learning-based dynamic resource provisioning for network slicing with ensured end-to-end performance bound. IEEE Trans. Netw. Sci. Eng. **7**(1), 28–41 (2020). https://doi.org/10.1109/TNSE.2018.2876918
13. Xylouris, G., et al.: Experimentation and 5G KPI measurements in the 5GENESIS platforms. In: Proceedings of the 1st Workshop on 5G Measurements, Modeling, and Use Cases, 5G-MeMU 2021, pp. 1–7. Association for Computing Machinery, New York (2021). https://doi.org/10.1145/3472771.3472776

Improving the Efficiency of WebRTC Layered Simulcast Using Software Defined Networking

Agnieszka Chodorek[1]📵, Robert R. Chodorek[2]([✉])📵, and Krzysztof Wajda[2]📵

[1] Kielce University of Technology, Al. 1000-lecia P.P. 7, 25-314 Kielce, Poland
`a.chodorek@tu.kielce.pl`
[2] The AGH University of Science and Technology, Al. Mickiewicza 30,
30-059 Krakow, Poland
`{chodorek,krzysztof.wajda}@agh.edu.pl`
`https://telekomunikacja.agh.edu.pl/`

Abstract. This study proposes a conference bridge that cooperates with both the WebRTC layered simulcast and the Software Defined Networking architecture in order to improve WebRTC video streaming. The proposed bridge divides the functionality of a classic Selective Forwarding Unit into two parts. The selection of layers is performed by the SDN controller and the forwarding of layered video is still accomplished by the bridge. The bridge and the SDN controller exchange data on the state of the transmitted video stream and the state of the network. The proposed solution was implemented in the Jitsi Videobridge and tested in the GEANT testbed network. The results showed that our solution significantly reduces problems related to available throughput overshooting, which is typical for layered simulcast.

Keywords: WebRTC · Software Defined Networking · OpenFlow system · Quality of Service

1 Introduction

Forced by the events of the last few years, the rapid development of telemedicine, e-learning and all kinds of telework has become both an opportunity and a challenge for multimedia communication technology. The emerging technology that was able to both seize the opportunity and meet the challenges is the Web Real-Time Communications (WebRTC) [1,2], which introduced native real-time communication to the web. It offers some interesting features supporting efficient multimedia communication, including layered simulcast.

This work was supported by the Polish Ministry of Science and Higher Education with the subvention funds of the Faculty of Computer Science, Electronics and Telecommunications of AGH University.

W. Wang and J. Wu (Eds.): BROADNETS 2023, LNICST 511, pp. 13–28, 2023.
https://doi.org/10.1007/978-3-031-40467-2_2

1.1 Simulcast

In the field of information and communication technologies (ICT), simulcast denotes simultaneous streaming of the same content, encoded to different formats, different bitrates, or (if layered codecs are used) to successive layers. So-created streams (layers) are directed to middleboxes that serve a recipient or group of recipients and intermediates in simulcast transmissions. Middleboxes are implemented as media servers or Selective Forwarding Units (SFUs).

Streams and sets of successive layers are selectively forwarded to the recipients, and selection is carried out by the congestion control mechanism. Depending on the implementation, the congestion controller can be placed in the receiver (receiver-driven simulcast) or in a middlebox (node-driven simulcast).

Let N be the total number of streams or layers. The controller dynamically chooses 1 of the N replicated streams (stream replication simulcast) or a set of M layers (layered simulcast) in order to achieve the best quality of transmitted media that the network is able to deliver. Layers are chosen successively, from 1 to M of N. The chosen stream or set of layers are re-sent by the SFU to the destination (see explanatory drawing showed in Fig. 1). The process of choosing the stream/layers is repeated according to changes to the network's state.

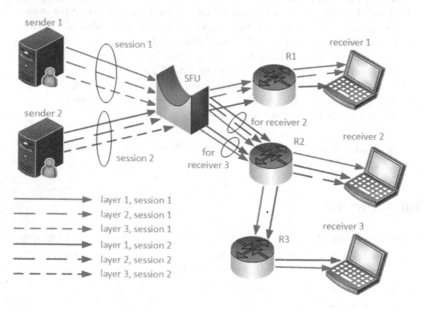

Fig. 1. The concept of layered simulcast. One SFU serves a group of recipients (receiver 1 to receiver 3).

1.2 WebRTC and WebRTC Simulcast

The WebRTC concept of native real-time communication in the Web was intended for peer-to-peer media communication between web browsers. However, the WebRTC-based conferencing system may be built as a centralized one, with the use of middleboxes (working as conferencing bridges). The most popular open source middleboxes, used by the WebRTC, are the Jitsi Meet, the Edumeet, the Kurento and the Simple Realtime Server (SRS). The comparison of WebRTC open source SFUs used for video conferencing is presented in this paper [3]. WebRTC is able to provide a conferencing service, when the conference bridge is placed in a computing cloud [4,5].

Currently, WebRTC is implemented in all popular web browsers, which are run-time environments for WebRTC applications. WebRTC applications are written according to the Single-Page Application (SPA) paradigm, with the use of the HyperText Markup Language (HTML) version 5 (HTML5) and the JavaScript language. WebRTC sessions are established using the JavaScript Session Establishment Protocol (JSEP) and the Session Description Protocol (SDP). Media (audio and video) are transmitted using the Real-time Transport Protocol (RTP) operating on a top of the User Datagram Protocol (UDP). The WebRTC has sophisticated congestion control of media streams, composed of several internal mechanisms. They are implemented in Web browsers, e.g. TCP-friendly Rate Control (TFRC), the Google Congestion Control (GCC), and in middleboxes. One of the congestion control mechanisms implemented in the middleboxes is simulcast. Performance evaluation of the congestion control implemented in Web browsers is presented in [6,7], and implemented in middleboxes as presented in [8,9].

Simulcast is a relatively new feature of the WebRTC derived from multicasting [10]. Initially, WebRTC applications were able to use classic simulcast, based on stream replication. Since January 2019 [11], the first browser that supported WebRTC was equipped with Scalable Video Coding (SVC) versions of popular codecs (the VP8, VP9, and H.264 codecs). In 2019, the W3C Editor's Draft enabled the use of layered simulcast, but significant work is still ongoing and is documented in subsequent versions of this draft. The latest version is dated 13 February 2023 [12].

1.3 Motivations, Contributions and Organization of This Paper

In the paper [8] it was reported that the WebRTC's simulcasts (both the stream replication one and the layered one) were not able to perform precise and fast reaction to congestion, even in wireless local area networks, where propagation delays are small. Lack of precise information about current path states and the trial-and-error evaluation of the available throughput causes overshooting of the estimation of available bandwidth, which leads to high error rates.

The aim of this paper is to show that this adverse phenomenon may be eliminated (or, at least, limited) by using knowledge of the current network state. Such knowledge is available in the Software Defined Network (SDN) switches. There are examples of cooperation between SDN and WebRTC in the literature (such as the use of WebRTC signalling information to allocate resources in the SDN network [13], SDN-assisted IP-multicasting in the 5G network ensuring effective distribution of WebRTC transmissions to multiple recipients [14], or building a distributed SFU using SDN [15]), but so far SDN has not been used for simulcast management.

The main contributions of this paper are:

– The concept of SDN-assisted simulcast management, designed to work with SFU managing WebRTC simulcast sessions.
– Evaluation of the prototype implementation of the proposed system in the GEANT testbed.

The rest of this paper is organized as follows. In the next section the concept of the proposed simulcast management system is described. Experiments aimed at the evaluation of this concept in the GEANT testbed network are presented in the third section. The fourth section shows and discusses results of performed experiments. The last, fifth section, briefly concludes this paper.

2   Related Work

This section discusses three aspects of related work: WebRTC architecture standards, research on WebRTC simulcast, and research on SDN support for WebRTC.

2.1   WebRTC Architecture and Use Cases

The main achievements of IETF RTCWeb WG are defining milestones for WebRTC and are summarized in basic RFCs defining WebRTC use cases [16], used video codecs [17] and audio codecs [18]. The main use cases listed in [16] are: the simple video communication service, screen sharing, file exchange, multiparty video communication, online game, and video conferencing systems. Examples of WebRTC applications shown in the literature cover the secure delivery of multimedia content [19], the video communication service [20], video conferencing [21], video collaboration [21] and multi-party videoconferencing [13,15]. WebRTC was also used in the Web of Things (WoT) systems for medical applications [5] and in the WoT-based flying monitoring systems [22–24].

A brief overview of WebRTC architecture and main features is included in [25,26], then extended in [27] and [28]. The concept of using simulcast, with a description of the architecture, implementation scenarios and mapping on SDP and RTP settings is presented in [29].

2.2   WebRTC Simulcast

Loreto and Romano describe a state-of-the-art of WebRTC standard ecosystem [10], and one of the sections of their paper is devoted to simulcasting as a probable part of WebRTC-1.0. The authors indicate that simulcast issues are still under discussion.

Lin et al. in the paper [30] showed that although simulcast allows for both high scalability and the building of cost-effective solutions, there are situations where resource utilization is suboptimal. As a solution to this problem, the authors proposed a global stream orchestration (GSO) using a controller with the full network information. With this knowledge, simulcast congestion control can omit sending simulcast streams that will not be received by any of the receivers.

Chodorek et al. in the paper [8] compare the adaptability and the congestion control ability of both variants of WebRTC simulcasting: stream replication simulcast and layered simulcast. Results showed that in a not-loaded (without background traffic) environment, where only static (infrastructural) limitations occur, both versions of simulcast give equally good QoS parameters. However, in the presence of competitive background traffic, layered simulcast gives greater throughput and lower error rates.

Grozev et al. in the paper [9] presented an experimental evaluation of the basic, stream replication simulcast, shown by the example of the teleconference, where each participant may send from one to three replicated streams. The stream replication simulcast was compared with a single-stream unicast. The authors also indicate the need of further research on WebRTC simulcasting.

Xhagjika et al. present in their work [31] a comparative study of WebRTC stream replication simulcast and unicast transmissions between end systems (WebRTC clients) and media servers located in computing clouds. Results show that simulcasting gives about a two times higher bit rate than congestion controlled (in a TCP-friendly manner) unicasting.

Bakar et al. in the paper [20] describes a mesh-connected WebRTC transmission system, in which a spatio-temporal layered simulcast is used. The original simulcast was supplemented by a proposed motion-adaptive layer selection algorithm. Results shows that the layered simulcast is beneficial for point-to-point mesh-connected WebRTC sessions. The authors in their next paper [32] extend their proposition to WebRTC sessions that use the SFU intermediate node.

Romano and Giangrande in the paper [33], and Romano et al. in the paper [19] describe an architecture envisaging a combination of multicast, simulcast and unicast communication scenarios in a hybrid, terrestrial-satellite network. Simulcasting may be used for adaptive streaming in a WebRTC-enabled access network.

2.3   SDN-Aided WebRTC

Real-time communication (RTC) video services require a network with personalized service delivery with a higher capacity and better QoE [34]. The SDN network allows for the cooperation with WebRTC to do that service.

Kirmizioglu et al. in the paper [13] describes a WebRTC videoconferencing system which uses scalable VP9 video. To provide QoS services WebRTC signalling goes to the Network Service Provider (NSP). The NSP operates over the SDN. All experiments are performed using Mininet.

Cox et al. in the paper [35] describe methods for detecting Rogue access points (RAPs) using the SDN network and the WebRTC architecture. All tests are performed using Mininet. Boubendir et al. in the paper [36] described SDN-enabled NFV for a Telco network. Analysis shows that network operators can offer special network processing and forwarding for WebRTC communication. In the paper [37] the same authors show that it is possible to create on-demand services for a WebRTC-based application (WebRTC-based applications demand services of the TURN server from a network provider, and the network provider sets it up on demand).

In the paper [14] written by Kirmizioglu et al., the service manager which reserves bandwidth between mesh-connected WebRTC clients according to the rates agreed by them was proposed. This solution works over the SDN network.

3   The Concept of the SDN-Assisted Layered Simulcast

In the case of the classic WebRTC layered simulcast, the SFU can act as a relay, which selectively forwards appropriate layers to the destination. The idea of the proposed SDN-assisted simulcast is to divide the functionality of a classic SFU into two parts. The first one is related to the layers' forwarding and multiplication. It still remains under the responsibility of the SFU. The second one, related to the layers' selection, is transferred to the SDN.

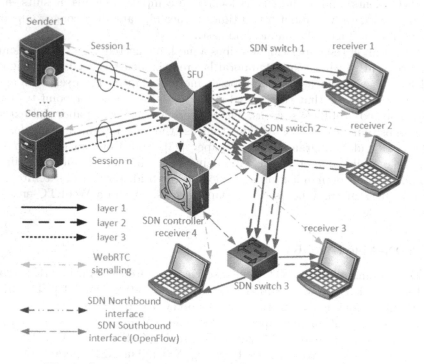

Fig. 2. General concept of the SDN-assisted layered simulcast.

The concept of an SDN-assisted layered simulcast is presented in Fig. 2. Senders performing the layered coding stream all the layers to the SFU, which multiplies them and forwards them non-selectively to the destinations. SDN switches in the path between the SFU and a given receiver block unnecessary layers. To avoid flooding of the network with unnecessary layers, switches that block them (SDN switch 1 and SDN switch 2) should be located as close the SFU as possible, preferably on the same network node as the SFU.

Under stable network conditions, unnecessary layers are not sent beyond the first switch in the path from the SFU to a given receiver. When increasing congestion is detected, the switches in the path block the transmission of the highest received layer (unless it is the base layer). The switch near the congested node also will block this layer forwarding and no packets of this layer will be injected into the congested area, even though some of them are still forwarded (see switch 3 and receiver 4 in Fig. 2).

The SDN network management is handled by the SDN controller, which has knowledge of the network topology and the current state of the network. The SDN controller is connected via the Northbound interface to the SFU from which it obtains information about the current state of the streamed media. On this basis, the SDN controller calculates the optimal number of layers that can be sent on the path between the SFU and a given receiver. The controller also gives feedback to the SFU about the current state of the network. The calculations of the number of layers that will be transmitted on the path from the sender to the receiver are performed according to Algorithm 1.

In the proposed solution, the SFU only coordinates all conferences in one site, providing signaling capabilities. Each SDN switch can act as the traditional SFU which select and forward desired layers.

4 Experiments

The proposed system was implemented in the Jitsi Videobridge [38] and SDN infrastructure of the multi-Gigabit European Academic NeTwork (GEANT). The Geant offers the Testbeds as a Service (TaaS) [39] service that uses eight nodes (Fig. 3), one each in Amsterdam, Bratislava, Hamburg, London, Madrid, Milano, Paris, and Prague. Each node includes a router (used to communicate with other nodes), an SDN switch supporting the OpenFlow protocol, and a local switch (used to communicate inside the node).

For the purposes of our experiments, the resources (bare metal servers, virtual servers and network equipment) of five nodes have been reserved. The conference bridge and a bulk traffic generator were placed in Paris. The WebRTC senders were placed in Amsterdam, London, and Hamburg. The WebRTC receiver was placed in Madrid, and the receiver of bulk data that were the background Transmission Control Protocol (TCP) traffic, as well. The SDN controller was placed in Paris, as was the conference bridge, which simplified the communication between these devices. SDN switches were placed on all eight network nodes.

As the software of a conference bridge, the Jitsi Videobridge that implements the proposed extensions was used. For comparison, the original Jitsi Videobridge, without our extensions, was used. During all experiments, default time constants of the Jitsi Videobridge were set.

Algorithm 1. Calculate available layers on the path

Require: conference poarticipant destination $ConfDst$, conference sender (source) $ConfSrc$

1: Initialize
2: $P \leftarrow GetPath(ConfSrc, ConfDst)$
3: $L \leftarrow GetLayers(ConfSrc)$
4: $c_{min} \leftarrow \infty$
5: **while** $p_i \in P$ **do** /* calulate avaiable capcity on on the path */
6:     $c_i \leftarrow EstimateAviableCapacity(p_i)$
7:     **if** $c_i > c_{min}$ **then**
8:         $c_{min} \leftarrow c_i$
9:     **end if**
10: **end while**
11: $layers \leftarrow 0$
12: $r_{total} \leftarrow 0$
13: **while** $l_i \in L$ **do**
14:     **if** $(r_{total} + Rate(l_i)) < c_{min}$ **then**
15:         $layers \leftarrow layers + 1$
16:         $r_{total} \leftarrow r_{total} + Rate(l_i)$
17:     **else**
18:         **return** layers
19:     **end if**
20: **end while**

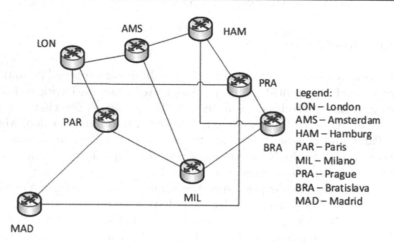

Fig. 3. Topology of GÉANT testbed. Distances between nodes have been preserved.

Video senders used the author's WebRTC application. Video from the camera was emulated by files of raw video information, both taken from a publicly available site [40] and captured as needed for this research (the latter includes the talking head of one of the authors, the parking lot of the AGH University, and a laboratory room). Video receivers used the author's WebRTC application.

For sake of comparison, the author's application of the receiver-driven layered multicast was also used. WebRTC applications used the Google Chrome browser as their run-time environment. In the case of the senders, Google Chrome was configured to use an external y4m file (video stream written in YUV4Mpeg format) as a video source instead of a camera. As the generator of TCP background traffic, the iperf tool [41] was used.

The links between the conference bridge and the senders were set to 100 Mbps, and the links between the bridge and the receivers were set to 2 Mbps or 10 Mbps (default for the GEANT testbed). The throughputs of the links between the bridge and the receivers were the same during a single experiment.

For the purposes of the evaluation of the proposed solution, three experiments were carried out. The first one was focused on static (infrastructural) limitations and their impact on a WebRTC layered simulcast. The next two were focused on dynamic constrains, introduced by layers competing for network resources (experiment 2) and by competing layers and TCP flows (experiment 3). The WebRTC senders had at their disposal 3 ($N = 3$) layers: the first one was the base layer, the second one was a spatial layer, and the third one was a temporal layer. The target bit rate (TBR) of the two first layers was equal to 0.6 Mbps, the third one to 1.2 Mbps, and the total TBR (i.e. TBR of the highest quality streaming video) was 2.4 Mbps.

5   Evaluation

The proposed solution was tested in three experiments, described in the previous section. Results of these experiments were compared with results obtained in corresponding experiments carried out in the same circumstances with the use of the WebRTC's receiver-driven layered simulcast.

5.1   Experiment 1: Single Video Streaming, No Background Traffic

Experiment 1 was aimed at checking the stability of the communication system and its ability to select the optimal number of simulcasted layers in the case of a lack of dynamic load. During the experiment, the layered sender placed in London streamed video to the SFU in Paris, and then the required layers were re-sent from the SFU in Paris to the receiver in Madrid. Distance between the bridge and the receiver was about 1200 km. This resulted in a propagation delay of about 6 ms. The throughput of links between the SFU and receivers was set to 2 Mbps, so the network was not able to transmit 2.4 Mbps of the total target bit rate. Because in this experiment only static (infrastructure) constraints should affect the layered simulcast, no background traffic was injected into the network, and simulcasted streams competed for throughput with themselves.

The results obtained using the proposed solution are shown in Fig. 4. About five seconds after starting the observation, Jitsi Videobridge switched on the base layer (layer 1), and about five seconds later, the spatial layer (layer 2) was also switched on (Fig. 4a). The total throughput of the first two layers is approximately 1.200 Mbps. This is much less than the throughput of the link (2 Mbps), so no errors were detected (Fig. 4b).

Lossless transmission means that after exceeding the next time limit, the Jitsi Videobridge will decide to attach the next layer. At this point, a classic simulcast-based congestion control mechanism (which estimates the current state of the network through trial and error) would switch on the time layer (i.e. layer 3). This would inevitably lead to packet loss. However, our solution makes the decision about switching on/off any layer on the basis of both the network topology, the bit rate of the incoming layers, and the available throughput. As a result, our solution did not enable layer 3 (Fig. 4a), so the video transmission remained lossless (Fig. 4b). The zero packet loss shown in Fig. 4b proves the correct response of the proposed congestion control mechanism, which, having knowledge of the traffic and network, always switches on only those layers that allow for the transmission of the highest possible total bit rate, provided that the total transmission rate does not exceed the throughput of the path between the transmitter and the receiver.

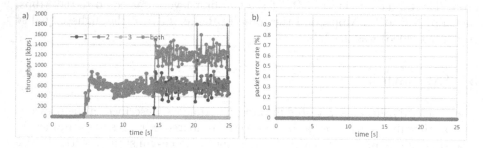

Fig. 4. Layered simulcast provided by the proposed solution: (a) throughput as a function of time, (b) packet error rate as a function of time.

For sake of comparison, the WebRTC simulcasting that use the original Jitsi Videobridge was tested in the same circumstances (Fig. 5). Due to the same Jitsi Videobridge settings, the first two layers were switched on at the same times (counting from the start of transmission) as in the case shown in Fig. 4. Since finding the available throughput is now a trial and error process, the temporal layer (layer 3) also was switched on. The cumulative throughput of the three layers exceeds 2 Mbps, which resulted in packet loss due to congestion. Although the layer 3 was soon switched off, unacceptably high (between 8 and 18 percent, median 12 percent) packet error rates (PERs) were observed for at least 5 s (Fig. 5b).

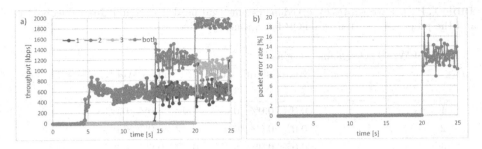

Fig. 5. Typical solution of WebRTC layered simulcast: (a) throughput as a function of time, (b) packet error rate as a function of time.

The trial-and-error evaluation of the available throughput means that, unlike the proposed solution, the layer 3 will be switched on every now and then, each time producing equally high error rates. Network neutrality, which results in non-discrimination of the transmitted layers, also resulted in packet loss not only in layer 3, but in all three layers. As a result, the quality of video transmission experienced by a user is unacceptable from time to time (in fact, the user then sees a still picture - the last properly received video frame).

5.2   Experiment 2: Multiple Video Streaming, No TCP Traffic

Experiments 2 was aimed at checking the system in terms of stability and the selection of layers in the presence of both static and dynamic constrains, while dynamic ones were introduced by multiple simulcast sessions. During this experiment, the receiver in Madrid participated in 1 to 5 simulcast sessions (each from 1 to 3 layers), established by the sender in London (1 session) and the senders in Amsterdam and Hamburg (each from 0 to 2 sessions). The throughput of links between the SFU and the receivers was set to 10 Mbps. The packet error rates that occurred during Experiment 2 are listed in Table 1.

When the number of WebRTC sessions was less than or equal to 2 (cumulative TBR less than half of 10 Mbps), no error was observed during transmission carried out with the use of both the proposed solution and the original Jitsi Videobridge (Table 1). Although the cumulative TBR of a single simulcast session (2.4 Mbps) should ensure the receipt of all 3 layers up to 4 sessions, the heterogeneity of footage available at [40] (movies with scene changes) causes temporary significant increase in traffic volume when changing scenes and then quick return to the set TBR. As a result, the increase in the number of sessions to 3 caused that the temporal layer (layer 3) was not able to be fully transmitted, and further increase in the number of sessions (to 4 and 5) caused both the spatial and temporal layers (layers 2 and 3) not to be fully transmitted through the network.

Table 1. Packet error rates observed in systems that used the original Jitsi Videobridge and the proposed solution. No TCP background traffic.

No. of WebRTC sessions	original			proposed		
	No. of simulcast stream within WebRTC session					
	1	2	3	1	2	3
1	0.0%	0.0%	0.0%	0.0%	0.0%	0.0%
2	0.0%	0.0%	0.0%	0.0%	0.0%	0.0%
3	0.0%	0.0%	5.1%	0.0%	0.0%	0.2%
4	0.0%	3.3%	11.4%	0.0%	0.1%	1.5%
5	0.0%	6.7%	20.2%	0.0%	0.4%	1.8%

This effect occurred when both the proposed solution and the original Jitsi Videobridge was used. However, when the proposed solution was used, the PER observed was one order of magnitude smaller than that of the original solution. In absolute terms, this resulted in an improvement of between 3.2 (4 sessions, 2 layers) and 18.4 (5 sessions, 3 layers) percentage points, and in relative terms, an improvement of 3 (4 sessions, 2 layers) to 13.2 (4 sessions, 3 layers) percent.

5.3   Experiment 3: Multiple Video Streaming, TCP Traffic

Experiment 3 extends the experiment 2 with presence of background bulk data traffic, transmitted with the use of the TCP. As a result, a given simulcast session has to adapt to static (infrastructural) limitations and to dynamic limitations introduced by both competing WebRTC sessions and TCP flows. The packet error rates that occurred during Experiment 3 are shown in Table 2.

Table 2. Packet error rates observed in systems that used the original Jitsi Videobridge and the proposed solution. TCP background traffic.

No. of WebRTC sessions	original			proposed		
	No. of simulcast stream within WebRTC session					
	1	2	3	1	2	3
1	0.0%	0.2%	0.5%	0.0%	0.1%	0.2%
2	0.1%	1.3%	3.2%	0.1%	0.2%	0.4%
3	0.1%	3.9%	7.3%	0.1%	0.3%	0.5%
4	0.1%	7.4%	11.5%	0.1%	0.4%	0.7%
5	0.2%	10.4%	15.2%	0.2%	0.4%	0.8%

Each session competed for link throughput with other sessions, as in experiment 2, and, additionally, with TCP traffic. As a result, error-free transmission was possible only in the case of a single base layer sharing the link with one TCP flow. In all other cases, the introduction of TCP background traffic caused that layers, including the base one, were not transmitted without errors.

When only the base layers were transmitted, simulcast congestion control was not possible, so the PERs only depended on the number of WebRTC sessions (the greater the number of sessions, the higher the PER), and was not dependent on simulcast management. As a result, the PERs observed when the proposed solution was used and the PERs observed when the original solution was used were equal to each other.

In the remaining cases, the packet error rate depended both on the number of WebRTC sessions (i.e. the number of layers competing for the throughput of the shared link) and the effectiveness of the congestion control mechanisms used. This time, the increase in PER as a function of the number of simulcast sessions, observed when the proposed solution was used, was significantly slower than the corresponding increase in PER observed when the original solution was used (Table 2). In particular, after using our solution, the packet error rate decreased two times for a single simulcast session, and for five simulcast sessions it decreased by two orders of magnitude. When the first two layers were switched on, the improvement was, in absolute terms, from 0.1 (1 session) to 10 (5 sessions) percentage points, and in relative terms, from 3.8 (5 sessions) to 50 (1 session) percent. When all three layers were switched on, the improvement was, in absolute terms, from 0.3 (1 session) to 14.4 (5 sessions) percentage points, and in relative terms, from 5.5 (5 sessions) to 40 (1 session) percent.

6   Conclusions

In this paper the SDN-assisted conference bridge acting as a SFU for a WebRTC layered simulcasting is proposed. Part of the SFU functionality (related to multiplication and forwarding of layered video) is accomplished by the bridge, while the other part (related to selection layers for forwarding purposes) is transferred to the SDN. During simulcast transmissions, the conference bridge gets data on the network state from the SDN controller, and the controller gets data on the state of the transmitted video from the bridge.

The results of the evaluation carried out in the GEANT testbed network showed that in the network not loaded with TCP traffic, but only with video traffic, packet error rates were up to 1.8%, and in the network loaded with TCP traffic, packet error rates were up to 0.8%. The worst-case error rates were observed for 5 simulcast sessions, each with 3 layers turned on, whose total target bit rate has exceeded the bottleneck throughput by 20%. In the same circumstances, the classic solution achieved PERs of 20.2%, and 15%, respectively.

In conclusion, the SDN controller included in the process of selecting layers depending on the current network state, is able to react quickly and autonomously. The use of both information about the network state and information about the WebRTC simulcast session sent from the SFU allowed the controller to avoid the misbehaviour of simulcasted transmissions when a new layer is switched on, caused by the overshooting of the estimation of available bandwidth, typical for classic solutions based on trial-and-error evaluation.

References

1. Loreto, S., Romano, S.P.: Real-Time Communication with WebRTC: Peer-to-Peer in the Browser. O'Reilly Media Inc. (2014)
2. Jennings, C., Boström, H., Bruaroey, J.: WebRTC 1.0: Real-Time Communication between Browsers; W3C Recommendation (2021). https://www.w3.org/TR/2021/REC-webrtc-20210126/. Accessed 15 Feb 2023
3. André, E., Le Breton, N., Lemesle, A., Roux, L., Gouaillard, A.: Comparative study of WebRTC open source SFUs for video conferencing. In: Proceedings of the 2018 Principles, Systems and Applications of IP Telecommunications (IPTComm), pp. 1–8 (2018)
4. López, L., et al.: Kurento: the WebRTC modular media server. In: Proceedings of the 24th ACM International Conference on Multimedia, pp. 1187–1191 (2016)
5. Chodorek, R.R., Chodorek, A., Rzym, G., Wajda, K.: A comparison of QoS parameters of WebRTC videoconference with conference bridge placed in private and public cloud. In: Proceedings of the IEEE 26th International Conference on Enabling Technologies: Infrastructure for Collaborative Enterprises (WETICE), pp. 86–91 (2017)
6. Chodorek, A., Chodorek, R.R., Wajda, K.: An analysis of sender-driven WebRTC congestion control coexisting with QoS assurance applied in IEEE 802.11 wireless LAN. In: Proceedings of the 2019 International Conference on Software, Telecommunications and Computer Networks (SoftCOM), pp. 1–5 (2019)
7. Singh, V., Lozano, A.A., Ott, J.: Performance analysis of receive-side real-time congestion control for WebRTC. In: Proceedings of the International Packet Video Workshop, pp. 1–8 (2013)
8. Chodorek, A., Chodorek, R.R., Wajda, K.: Comparison study of the adaptability of layered and stream replication variants of the WebRTC simulcast. In: Proceedings of the International Conference on Software, Telecommunications and Computer Networks (SoftCOM), pp. 1–6 (2019)
9. Grozev, B., Politis, G., Ivov, E., Noel, T., Singh, V.: Experimental evaluation of simulcast for WebRTC. IEEE Commun. Standards Mag. **1**(2), 52–59 (2017)
10. Loreto, S., Romano, S.P.: How far are we from WebRTC-1.0? An update on standards and a look at what's next. IEEE Commun. Mag. **55**(7), 200–207 (2017)
11. Uberti, J.: Simulcast encoding is now supported in @webrtc for the VP8, VP9, and H.264 codecs - try it out using the latest Chrome Canary, on Twitter (2019). https://twitter.com/juberti/status/1085764367113572353. Accessed 15 Feb 2023
12. Scalable Video Coding (SVC) Extension for WebRTC, W3C Editor's Draft (2023). https://w3c.github.io/webrtc-svc/. Accessed 15 Feb 2023
13. Kirmizioglu, R.A., Kaya, B.C., Tekalp, A.M.: Multi-party WebRTC videoconferencing using scalable VP9 video: from best-effort over-the-top to managed value-added services. In: Proceedings of the 2018 IEEE International Conference on Multimedia and Expo (ICME), pp. 1–6 (2018)
14. Kirmizioglu, R.A., Tekalp, A.M.: Multi-party WebRTC services using delay and bandwidth aware SDN-assisted IP multicasting of scalable video over 5G networks. IEEE Trans. Multimed. **22**(1), 1005–1015 (2019)
15. Kirmizioglu, R.A., Tekalp, A.M., Görkemli, B.: Distributed Virtual Selective-Forwarding Units and SDN-Assisted Edge Computing for Optimization of Multi-party WebRTC Videoconferencing (2022). Available at SSRN. https://ssrn.com/abstract=4045902 (Preprint submitted to Signal Processing: Image Communication). Accessed 15 Feb 2023

16. Holmberg, Ch., Eriksson, G., Hakansson, S.: Web Real-Time Communication Use Cases and Requirements. RFC 7478, IETF (2015)
17. Roach, A.: WebRTC Video Processing and Codec Requirements. RFC 7742, IETF (2016)
18. Valin, J.M., Bran, C.: WebRTC Audio Codec and Processing Requirements. RFC 7874, IETF (2016)
19. Romano, S.P., Roseti, C., Tulino, A.M.: SHINE: secure hybrid in network caching environment. In: Proceedings of the 2018 International Symposium on Networks, Computers and Communications (ISNCC), pp. 1–6 (2018)
20. Bakar, G., Kirmizioglu, R.A., Tekalp, A.M.: Motion-based adaptive streaming in WebRTC using spatio-temporal scalable VP9 video coding. In: 2017 IEEE Global Communications Conference, GLOBECOM 2017, pp. 1–6 (2017)
21. Petrangeli, S., Pauwels, D., van der Hooft, J., Wauters, T., De Turck, F., Slowack, J.: Improving quality and scalability of WebRTC video collaboration applications. In: Proceedings of the 9th ACM Multimedia Systems Conference, pp. 533–536 (2018)
22. Chodorek, A., Chodorek, R.R., Wajda, K.: Media and non-media WebRTC communication between a terrestrial station and a drone: the case of a flying IoT system to monitor parking. In: Proceedings of the 2019 IEEE/ACM 23rd International Symposium on Distributed Simulation and Real Time Applications (DS-RT), pp. 1–4 (2019)
23. Chodorek, A., Chodorek, R.R., Yastrebov, A.: The prototype monitoring system for pollution sensing and online visualization with the use of a UAV and a WebRTC-based platform. Sensors 22(4), 1578 (2022)
24. Chodorek, A., Chodorek, R.R., Yastrebov, A.: Weather sensing in an urban environment with the use of a UAV and WebRTC-based platform: a pilot study. Sensors 21(21), 7113 (2021)
25. Loreto, S., Romano, S.P.: Real-time communications in the web: Issues, achievements, and ongoing standardization efforts. IEEE Internet Comput. 16(5), 68–73 (2012)
26. Blum, N., Lachapelle, S., Alvestrand, H.: WebRTC-realtime communication for the open web platform: what was once a way to bring audio and video to the web has expanded into more use cases we could ever imagine. Queue 19(1), 77–93 (2021)
27. Amirante, A., Castaldi, T., Miniero, L., Romano, S.P.: On the seamless interaction between webRTC browsers and SIP-based conferencing systems. IEEE Commun. Mag. 51(4), 42–47 (2013)
28. Johnston, A., Yoakum, J., Singh, K.: Taking on webRTC in an enterprise. IEEE Commun. Mag. 51(4), 48–54 (2013)
29. Burman, F., Westerlund, M., Nandakumar, S., Zanaty, M.: Using Simulcast in Session Description Protocol (SDP) and RTP Sessions. RFC 8853, IETF (2021)
30. Lin, X., et al.: GSO-simulcast: global stream orchestration in simulcast video conferencing systems. In: Proceedings of the ACM SIGCOMM 2022 Conference, pp. 826–839 (2022)
31. Xhagjika, V., Escoda, O.D., Navarro, L., Vlassov, V.: Media streams allocation and load patterns for a WebRTC cloud architecture. In: Proceedings of the 8th International Conference on the Network of the Future (NOF), pp. 14–21 (2017)
32. Bakar, G., Kirmizioglu, R.A., Tekalp, A.M.: Motion-based rate adaptation in WebRTC videoconferencing using scalable video coding. IEEE Trans. Multimed. 21(2), 429–441 (2018)

33. Romano, S.P., Giangrande, F.: On the use of network coding as a virtual network function in satellite-terrestrial CDNs. In: Proceedings of the IEEE INFOCOM 2018-IEEE Conference on Computer Communications Workshops (INFOCOM WKSHPS), pp. 662–667 (2018)
34. Jero, S., Gurbani, V.K., Miller, R., Cilli, B., Payette, C., Sharma, S.: Dynamic control of real-time communication (RTC) using SDN: a case study of a 5G end-to-end service. In: Proceedings of the NOMS 2016–2016 IEEE/IFIP Network Operations and Management Symposium, pp. 895–900 (2016)
35. Cox, J.H., Clark, R., Owen, H.: Leveraging SDN and WebRTC for rogue access point security. IEEE Trans. Netw. Serv. Manag. **14**(3), 756–770 (2017)
36. Boubendir, A., Bertin, E., Simoni, N.: Network as-a-service: the WebRTC case: how SDN & NFV set a solid Telco-OTT groundwork. In: Proceedings of the 2015 6th International Conference on the Network of the Future (NOF), pp. 1–3 (2015)
37. Boubendir, A., Bertin, E., Simoni, N.: On-demand dynamic network service deployment over NaaS architecture. In: Proceedings of the NOMS 2016–2016 IEEE/IFIP Network Operations and Management Symposium, pp. 1023–1024 (2016)
38. Jitsi Videobridge. https://jitsi.org/jitsi-videobridge/. Accessed 15 Feb 2023
39. Farina, F., Szegedi, P., Sobieski, J.: GÉANT world testbed facility: federated and distributed testbeds as a service facility of GÉANT. In: Proceedings of the 26th International Teletraffic Congress (ITC), pp. 1–6 (2014)
40. Xiph.org Video Test Media [Derf's collection]. https://media.xiph.org/video/derf/. Accessed 15 Feb 2023
41. iPerf. https://iperf.fr/. Accessed 15 Feb 2023

Mobile Software Security

Deep CounterStrike: Counter Adversarial Deep Reinforcement Learning for Defense Against Metamorphic Ransomware Swarm Attack

Mohit Sewak[1]([⊠]), Sanjay K. Sahay[2], and Hemant Rathore[2]

[1] Security and Compliance Research, Microsoft R&D India Pvt. Ltd.,
Hyderabad, India
mohit.sewak@microsoft.com
[2] Department of CS&IS, BITS Pilani, K K Birla Goa Campus, Goa, India
{ssahay,hemantr}@goa.bits-pilani.ac.in

Abstract. Ransomware, create a devastating impact when it infects a system. Fortunately, post the initial breach, such ransomware could be detected using advanced machine learning techniques, and therefore other high-value assets/systems can be protected from any repeat attack by the same ransomware. However, using metamorphism, advanced/ second-generation ransomware can alter its structure after every successful infection. With this ability of metamorphism, such advanced ransomware could continue to evade any defensive mechanism and keep infecting systems in subsequent networks. Currently, there exists neither any proven defensive mechanism nor any useful dataset to train a defensive mechanism against such advanced ransomware. Therefore, we present a deep counter adversarial reinforcement learning-based system that learns how to normalize the metamorphism of such advanced ransomware to design a credible defence against such advanced attacks. To augment training data for this system, we design and develop a deep adversarial reinforcement learning solution, to generate swarms of such advanced ransomware.

Keywords: Deep Reinforcement Learning · Adversarial Learning · Ransomware · Metamorphic Malware · Swarm Attack

1 Introduction

Ransomware is a type of malware that can infect/encrypt the system for ransom. In this, the recent/advanced ransomware developer uses obfuscation techniques to change its structure after every attack/infection/system encryption [2,21] to evade the deployed malware defence system. To detect ransomware, generally, samples are collected during the forensics of the compromised machines. From the collected samples, signatures are extracted and submitted to various malware defence systems to safeguard other machines across the networksv [21,32].

© ICST Institute for Computer Sciences, Social Informatics and Telecommunications Engineering 2023
Published by Springer Nature Switzerland AG 2023. All Rights Reserved
W. Wang and J. Wu (Eds.): BROADNETS 2023, LNICST 511, pp. 31–50, 2023.
https://doi.org/10.1007/978-3-031-40467-2_3

But such mechanisms fail to mitigate the attacks from advanced/metamorphic ransomware because such ransomware alters its structure after the infection, and the resulting obfuscated ransomware is not often identified by the malware defence system that was trained on original/similar ransomware samples.

Fortunately, it is challenging to design and develop obfuscated ransomware. But what if such ransomware could be generated through Artificial Intelligence (AI); and not just single ransomware, but a swarm of these to target a system? Therefore, to pro-actively defend/detect the advanced ransomware, in this paper, we first introduce an AI system to infuse metamorphic capabilities into existing base variants of ransomware and other malware. We show that augmented with such metamorphic capabilities, ransomware could evade even the most advanced and highly sophisticated machine learning (ML) and deep learning (DL) malware detection systems. Such evasion is broadly covered in literature as *adversarial* learning. But, the available literature on Adversarial-DL/ML attacks mostly works by adding strategic noise for evading DL classifiers. Therefore, such mechanisms are not suitable for our purpose because the resulting file may not replicate the functionality of ransomware. Also, such a file may not even be re-package-able to a valid executable program. Another aspect to consider in security is that adversarially robust malware detectors are popular. Hence, the malware classifiers may use algorithms that are immune to gradient-attacks [7] and other adversarial-DL/ML attacks [17]. Therefore, adversarial-DL/ML-based mechanisms cannot generate samples that can effectively and consistently evade existing adversarial-DL-immune malware detectors. Thus, using Adversarial-DL/ML-based solutions is not ideal for the purpose, and accordingly, one has to look forward to Reinforcement Learning (RL) based approaches. However, RL and even popular Deep Reinforcement Learning (DRL) algorithms [28,37] could not handle large action spaces. Therefore, in this paper, first, we develop Adversarial Deep Reinforcement Learning (A-DRL) using complex Proximal Policy Optimization (PPO) [26], which obfuscates malware using techniques like junk-code insertion.

The developed model modifies the sequence and frequency vectors of the opcodes as extracted from the disassembled ransomware while preserving their malicious capabilities and other functionalities, which to the best of our knowledge, there exists no evidence in open literature which counter the attack from such advanced metamorphic ransomware and any attack that has used advanced metamorphic ransomware. Therefore, first, we describe how we succeeded in creating such ransomware samples and also trained multiple diversely instantiated Adversarial Deep Reinforcement Learning (A-DRL) agents, each of which could create a unique metamorphic variant of base ransomware. Collectively, so many obfuscated variants of ransomware created a swarm of advanced, second-generation, metamorphic ransomware. Finally, we propose a defence called Counter-Adversarial-DRL (C-A-DRL) system which probably will be the first solution to defend against any such extreme attacks.

The C-A-DRL system will solve the problem of defence against metamorphic ransomware by normalizing the obfuscations in any metamorphic malware and thereby transforming them into their base variant, which is more likely to be detectable by an existing malware detection system. The C-A-DRL is also based on deep policy-based RL [26,30]. Still, it uses even more computationally complex learning mechanisms to solve the more complex problem of normalizing the malware.

The rest of the paper is organized as follows. Section 2 covers related work in A-DL, malware detection and evasion. Section 3 provides the rationale for designing a counter-adversarial system instead of re-training the detection system with adversarial data. Next, Sect. 4 describes the two different DRL environments used. Section 5 covers the mathematical lineage of the algorithms. Section 6 describes the dataset, features, and challenger malware detection systems assessed for use within the DRL environments. Section 7 and 8 explain the experiments conducted and the results. Finally, we conclude the paper in Sect. 9.

2   Related Work

Adversarial attack on security systems is a trending topic in both AI and security research. In the AI research, Generative Adversarial Networks [6,36] have made A-DL exceedingly popular. Subsequently, this science started being misused for various purposes. With injections of random/noisy perturbations into detection candidate feature tensors, a DL classifier could be fooled to miss-classify even simple candidates [17]. This phenomenon is known as *adversarial attack* in DL [9, 39]. In efforts to counter such attacks, some interesting ideas have been proposed in [10,11,20,24].

Some researchers have identified the drawbacks in the design of perturbations-based adversarial-DL mechanisms in security and have started using alternate techniques. Some researchers have used techniques like the classical RL [19], while some others have even proposed value-based DRL algorithms like the Deep Q Networks (DQN) [22] to perpetuate such adversarial attacks on network traffic. But most of these systems work at the same or similarly abstracted feature level where no actual malware could be practically created as any operating system compatible file, even if it could theoretically be re-assembled and re-packaged after such modifications. To the best of our knowledge, we are not aware of any system that could re-package a modified file to an actual executable that could infect any system (or even preserve any functionality).

Recently, ransomware attacks [5,15], especially those involving human-operated ransomware (HumOR) have increased, both in frequency and impact to become the predominant threat. As metamorphic malware could change its structure after every infection, therefore it is difficult to detect using conventional methods [18,35]. Where ransomware and metamorphic malware [1,34] are the most dreadful threat vectors, the zero-day attacks [3], and swarm attacks are the most dreadful attack scenarios.

3   Rationale for a Ransomware Normalization Based Defence Mechanism

As ransomware defenders, we regularly encounter two main challenges. First is the availability of quality ransomware data in large volumes to train a modern DL-based classifier. The second is the discovery of an effective DL architecture that could be trained to detect ransomware using the extracted features from the available dataset. But unfortunately, the second approach will not be conducive to the purpose of evading a metamorphic attack. This is because we started with the premise that the PPO-based DRL adversary agents could learn to evade most of the classifiers. Evading another DL classifier, even the ones re-trained with existing adversarial data, would be as trivial as playing some more episodes for the A-DRL agent. Hence, such an approach is not only counterproductive but also highly risky, as in a zero-day swarm attack scenario, ML/DL-based classifiers are prone to false-negative. Moreover, even if we re-train a new classifier with adversarial data, it has two main drawbacks. First, training a classifier with adversarial data renders the resulting classifier vulnerable to gradient attacks. Second, over-sampling of data that otherwise represents a small subset of existing ransomware makes the classifier over-fit to these samples, and thereby reduces the classifier's effectiveness. Therefore, ideally, we would like to design a defence mechanism that does not involve any training with adversarial data. Further, we would like only minimal changes to any other sub-component of the endpoint detection system. Alternatively, a better approach would be to use a malware normalization pre-processor. As opposed to retraining an existing detection system, an additional pre-processing by a malware normalization system works by de-obfuscating the obfuscated metamorphic malware to its base form and hence will be an ideal design for a defence mechanism.

4   A-DRL and C-A-DRL Environment's Architecture

A schematic and the internal working flow of the A-DRL and C-A-DRL environment architecture to train the A-DRL agent for the generation of metamorphic variants of any malware is shown in Fig. 1. The architecture consists of seven components and is briefly described below:

1. Malware Repository: A repository of existing malware, which contains either the first generation or the base variant (or the ones for which the lineage could otherwise not be traced further) of available advanced metamorphic malware.
2. Malware Classification Sub-System: A complete malware detection/ classification pipeline of the malware detection system (covered in Sect. 6.1) with the most robust and performant detection on the associated malware repository.
3. Reward Function Computation: A component to compute the instantaneous reward at each step as per the reward function (discussed later in this section). Any subsequent discounting of these rewards (for attributing future rewards) is controlled by the agent algorithm.

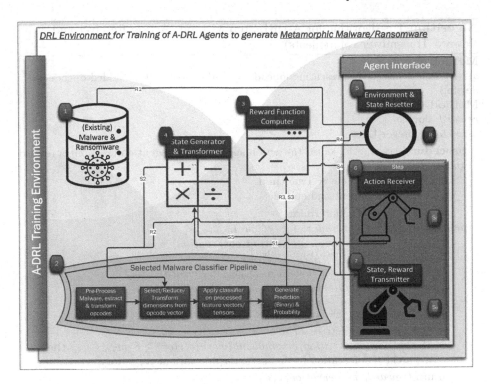

Fig. 1. Working flow of the A-DRL and C-A-DRL environment architecture.

4. State Generator and Transformer: This component uses the opcode feature vector modification suggestion from the agent to generate the next state corresponding to the agent's recommendations.
5. Environment and State Resetter: When an agent initiates a new training episode, it invokes this component functionality to reset the environment, the reward function, and the state vector.
6. Action Receiver: The action receiver along with the 'State Reward Transmitter' (component 7) constitutes the 'Step' functionality for the agent. The action-receiver receives the opcode feature modification suggestions from the agent as action and invokes the step method functionality as given in the Algorithm 1.
7. State Reward Transmitter: After processing the agent's action as per Algorithm 1, this component collects the generated rewards, and the resultant transformed state-vector corresponding to the suggested action and returns these to the agent to update its policy and recommend the action for the next step.

Algorithm 1 : Algorithm for A-DRL Step Method (Action Receiver and State Reward Transmitter components).

Method Input:

$action\_index$: integer (representing [opcode to add in sequence] +[added opcode to delete])

Method Output:

$reward$: double

new_state: integer$[1...M_O]$

    procedure STEP   ▷ Executes the action suggestion by agent and computes reward and next-state

        if $is\_episode\_complete$ = True **then**

            $reset\_environment\_and\_episode()$

      $new\_observation[action\_index] \leftarrow$

$new\_observation[action\_index] + / - Count_{Constant}$

      $\mathbb{P}_{NDMF} \leftarrow IsMalware_{Predict}(current\_observation)$

      $Reward_{Evasion} \leftarrow f(\mathbb{P}_{NDMF}^{Criteria1}, \mathbb{P}_{NDMF}^{Criteria2})$

      $Reward_{Discounted} \leftarrow \gamma * Reward_{Discounted} + Reward_{Evasion}$

      $Episode\_Turn\_Counter \leftarrow Episode\_Turn\_Counter + 1$

      $current\_observation \leftarrow new\_observation$

      if $\mathbb{P}_{NDMF} \geq P_{NDMF}^{threshold}$ **then**

         $is\_episode\_complete \leftarrow True$

         if $sim(new\_observation, original\_malware\_vector) \geq Sim_{Threshold}$ **then**

            archive obfuscation to the metamorphic variant repository

      return $(reward_t, nobservation_{t+1})$

The environment for the training of C-A-DRL is like that of the A-DRL, except for the malware repository and the reward computation module. Where the environment for the training of A-DRL contains a repository of all existing ransomware, the corresponding environment for the C-A-DRL system contains a repository of second-generation metamorphic ransomware. The reward functions for both environments are mathematically explained in Subsect. 4.1.

4.1 Reward Functions

We have at least two objectives for both the A-DRL and C-A-DRL agents. For A-DRL, the first objective is that it should be able to create enough ambiguity in the detection of the metamorphic variant. Because for most unbiased binary classifiers, the ambiguity point is at a probability of 0.5 (Eq. 1), we would like that the first aspect of the reward function to focus on this objective. This is translated as reward-criteria in the reward function as given in Eq. 2.

$$\mathbb{P}(AmbiguousDetection) =$$
$$\mathbb{P}(File_{Ransomware} \mid File \subseteq \{Ransomware\}) = \qquad (1)$$
$$\mathbb{P}(File_{Ransomware} \mid File \subseteq \{Non\text{-}Ransomware\}) = 0.5$$

$$\mathbb{R}_{\text{criteria-1}} : \mathbb{P}(\text{Detection}) = \mathbb{P}(\text{File}_{\text{Ransomware}})$$
$$<= \mathbb{P}(\text{AmbiguousDetection})$$
$$\mathbb{R}_1 = \mathbb{P}(\text{AmbiguousDetection}) - \mathbb{P}(\text{Detection}) \tag{2}$$
$$or, \mathbb{R}_1 = 0.5 - \mathbb{P}(\text{Detection})$$

The first reward criterion ensures that the agent learns to transform a definite ransomware detection into an ambiguous detection and, subsequently, a probable evasion. But, with this reward criterion in isolation, the agent will learn only to maintain $\mathbb{P}(\text{Detection}) < 0.5$ and thereby keep accumulating rewards. Whereas our main goal is to metamorph the ransomware to such an extent that it could be unambiguously detected as non-malicious. Also, we want to attain this in the minimum number of turns. However, the first aspect is partially, and the second aspect is completely missing in reward criterion 1. Therefore, we introduce another reward criterion, which gets triggered only when the detection probability reaches a higher threshold (say $\mathbb{P}(\text{File}_{\text{Ransomware}}) < 0.1$), and thereby generates a disproportionate higher reward. It is given in Eq. 3.

$$\mathbb{R}_{\text{criteria-2}} : \mathbb{P}(\text{Detection}) = \mathbb{P}(\text{File}_{\text{Ransomware}})$$
$$\leq \mathbb{P}_{\text{Threshold}} = 0.1$$
$$\mathbb{R}_2 = F(\text{Turns}_{Max}) = \text{Turns}_{Max} \times \delta \tag{3}$$
$$= \text{Turns}_{Max} \times \mathbb{P}(\text{AmbiguousDetection})$$

In Eq. 3, we kept the ultimate-objective reward as a function of Turns_{Max} (maximum number of turns allowed to the agent for a candidate file). This is to balance two opposing factors as under:

1. We want to have this reward disproportionately high enough such that the agent would weigh quicker termination more favourably than hunting in a range $\mathbb{P}(\text{File}_{\text{Ransomware}}) < 0.5$.
2. In cases where the agent is not able to reach this disproportionately high reward, it should still try to achieve reward criteria 1 and maintain it instead of completely disregarding it.

Here detection probability of ≤ 0.1 has been kept as the threshold to indicate unambiguous detection.

Another aspect in Eq. 3 is the constant multiplier δ, which is kept as $\mathbb{P}(\text{AmbiguousDetection})$ to enhance the balance against the reward-criteria 1 further. Combining these reward criteria, the final reward function ($\mathcal{R}_{\text{A-DRL}}$) is given in the Eq. 4.

$$\mathcal{R}_{\text{A-DRL}} = \begin{cases} 0.5 - \mathbb{P}(\text{Detection}), & \text{if } \mathbb{P}(\text{Detection}) \\ & \geq \mathbb{P}_{\text{Threshold}} \\ \text{Turns}_{Max} \times \delta, & \text{otherwise} \end{cases} \tag{4}$$

For the C-A-DRL agents, there are similar constraints as that of A-DRL, but their directions and limits change. Since we start from the ransomware samples generated corresponding to Eq. 2, for reward-criteria 1 for C-A-DRL, their default non-ambiguous probability range does not start at 0.0. Accordingly, the first reward criteria for C-A-DRL is given in the Eq. 5.

$$
\begin{aligned}
\mathbb{P}(\text{AmbiguousDetection})_{\text{C-A-DRL}} &= \\
\mathbb{P}(\text{File}_{\text{Ransomware}} \mid File \subseteq \{\text{Ransomware}\}) &= \\
\mathbb{P}(\text{File}_{\text{Ambiguous\_A-DRL}} \mid File \subseteq \{\text{Non-Ransomware}\}) & \\
&= 0.75 \\
\mathbb{R}_{\text{criteria-1}} : \mathbb{P}(\text{Detection}) &= \mathbb{P}(\text{File}_{\text{Ransomware}}) \\
&\geq \mathbb{P}(\text{AmbiguousDetection})_{\text{C-A-DRL}} \\
\mathbb{R}_1 = \mathbb{P}(\text{Detection}) &- \mathbb{P}(\text{AmbiguousDetection})_{\text{C-A-DRL}} \\
or, \mathbb{R}_1 &= \mathbb{P}(\text{Detection}) - 0.75
\end{aligned}
\tag{5}
$$

The reward-criteria 2 remains the same for C-A-DRL, except for the threshold for the criteria-trigger which becomes $\mathbb{P}_{\text{Threshold\_C-A-DRL}} = \mathbb{P}(\text{File}_{\text{Ransomware}} \mid File \subseteq \{\text{Ransomware}\}) - \mathbb{P}_{\text{Threshold\_A-DRL}} = 0.9$. Combining the reward criteria, the reward function for C-A-DRL is given in the Eq. 6.

$$
\mathcal{R}_{\text{C-A-DRL}} =
\begin{cases}
\mathbb{P}(\text{Detection}) - 0.75, & \text{if } \mathbb{P}(\text{Detection}) \\
& \geq \mathbb{P}_{\text{Th.\_C-A-DRL}} \\
\text{Turns}_{Max} \times \delta, & \text{otherwise}
\end{cases}
\tag{6}
$$

5   A-DRL and C-A-DRL Agent(s) Based on PPO Algorithm

Figure 2 shows the interaction between the A-DRL system's agent with its environment (via the agent interface) as per the training process. The C-A-DRL agent also similarly interacts with its environment.

The action space of the Markov Decision Process (MDP) for both the A-DRL and C-A-DRL problems consists of a vector of instruction set for the underlying kernel and processor platform. This makes the MDP for both of our DRL environments constrained to an exceptionally large cardinality discrete action space. As compared to classical RL/DRL, which could handle large state spaces very efficiently. Popular value-based DRL [27] algorithms like the DQN [13,14] and variants [8,40] claims to handle states representing multiple image-frame in Convolution Neural Network [29] tensors. Still, these also do not scale appropriately to accommodate high cardinality action spaces. Therefore, we appraised several policy-based DRL algorithms and finally used the PPO-based algorithm.

A policy-approximation-based algorithm needs to compute the expectancy of a particular policy to formulate the policy-utility function, for which it intends to find the gradient. The policy gradient for a Stochastic Policy Gradient [38] is

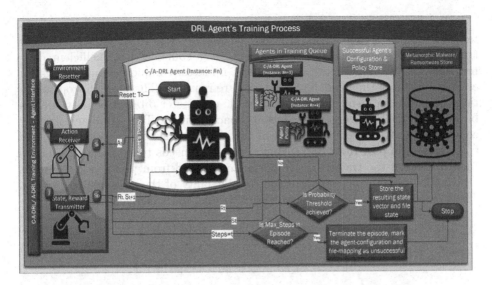

Fig. 2. DRL system's agent interaction with the environment.

given in Eq. 7, in which J is the policy-utility function that needs to be maximized and to maximize it, we need to compute the gradient ∇ of the policy-utility function. This requires finding expectancy $\mathbb{E}$ over different trajectories τ under this policy. Here $r(\tau)$ represents reward in trajectories parameterized by τ over which the expectancy is computed, and the one which is updated based on the resulting expectancy, and thereby the gradient of the policy-utility function.

$$\nabla_\theta(J_\theta) = \mathbb{E}_{\tau \sim \pi_\theta(\tau)}[\nabla_\theta \log \pi_\theta(\tau) r(\tau)] \qquad (7)$$

A very potent policy-based algorithm Trust Region Policy Optimization (TRPO) [25] instead samples expectancy from these trajectories differently as $\pi_{\theta\prime}$, and π_θ, and use their ratio as an additional term in the gradient of the utility function. Such a gradient is given in Eq. 8.

$$\nabla_{\theta\prime}(J_{\theta\prime}) = \mathbb{E}_{\tau \sim \pi_\theta(\tau)}[\sum_{t=1}^{T} \nabla_{\theta\prime} \log \pi_{\theta\prime}(\prod_{t\prime=1}^{t} \frac{\pi_{\theta\prime}}{\pi_\theta})(\sum_{t\prime=t}^{T} r)] \qquad (8)$$

To define the trust region and ensure that the updates are confined to this region, TRPO adds additional penalties to the optimization function to make the updates nearly monotonically, improving the utility function. With this, the optimization function for the gradient of J is given in Eq. 9.

$$\max_\theta \hat{\mathbb{E}}_t[\frac{\pi_\theta(a_t|s_t)}{\pi_{\theta old}(a_t|s_t)}\hat{A}_t - \beta.\mathrm{KL}[\pi_{\theta old}(.|s_t), \pi_\theta(.|s_t)]] \qquad (9)$$

Here, a_t is the action corresponding to the states s_t at time t, r_t is the instantaneous reward at time t and $\hat{A}_t$ is the Advantage. The Eq. 9 parameterize the trust-region penalties with a coefficient β. This could lead to inefficient optimization, as before computing any policy updates, complex computations for establishing an optimal value of β update are required. Therefore, for optimization computation, instead of the optimizable parameter β based penalty, a Kullback Leibler (KL) divergence-based approach is used. This approach directly computes the KL divergence between the distributions of $\pi_{\theta\prime}$ (distribution of trajectories sampled from the current policy that needs to be updated) and π_θ (distribution of the trajectories importance-sampled from previous policies) as a proxy for the limiting conditions for applicability of the trust-region bounds. The simpler optimization problem with KL constraints is given in Eq. 10.

$$\max_\theta \hat{\mathbb{E}}_t[\frac{\pi_\theta(a_t|s_t)}{\pi_{\theta old}(a_t|s_t)}\hat{A}_t] \tag{10}$$
$$\text{subject to } \hat{\mathbb{E}}_t[\text{KL}[\pi_{\theta old}(.|s_t), \pi_\theta(.|s_t)]] \le \delta.$$

The PPO algorithm offers a more efficient solution to implement the KL penalty constraint for optimization under the trust-region bounds. The PPO algorithm removes the KL penalties from the optimization function and simplifies the associated updates. Instead of using the KL penalties, it clips the surrogate objective as given in Eq. 11, ensuring that the updates are not completely unbound.

$$L^{CPI}(\theta) = \hat{\mathbb{E}}_t[\frac{\pi_\theta(a_t|s_t)}{\pi_{\theta old}(a_t|s_t)}\hat{A}_t] = \hat{\mathbb{E}}_t[r_t(\theta)\hat{A}_t]. \tag{11}$$

The original surrogate objective L^{CPI} in the 'clipped' form as used in TRPO can be reformulated and is given in the Eq. 12, where, ϵ (with a default value of 0.2) is an adjustable hyper-parameter.

$$L^{CLIP}(\theta) = \hat{\mathbb{E}}_t[\min(r_t(\theta)\hat{A}_t, clip(r_t(\theta), 1 - \epsilon, 1 + \epsilon)\hat{A}_t)]. \tag{12}$$

Alternatively, Eq. 13 provides another mechanism as a replacement for the KL divergence-based penalty for optimization. In this alternative mechanism, instead of replacing the optimizable β parameter with KL penalties, an adaptive β penalty is used. Experimental results, though, favour the clipped penalty variant (Eq. 12) over the adaptive penalty variant as given in Eq. 13. Hence, most practical applications of PPO default to the clipped KL penalty forms for the implementation of the PPO algorithm. We also use this form of PPO algorithm implementation as the agents for both the A-DRL and C-A-DRL systems.

$$\beta = \begin{cases} \beta/2, & \text{if } d \le d_{targ}/1.5 \\ \beta \times 2, & \text{if } d \ge d_{targ} \times 1.5 \\ \beta & \text{otherwise} \end{cases} \tag{13}$$
$$\text{where, } d = \hat{\mathbb{E}}_t[KL[\pi_\theta(.|s_t), \pi_{\theta old}(.|s_t)]]$$

PPO uses the popular actor-critic [12,23] framework for implementation, with options of DL models for service as actor and critic. We use a DNN with hidden layers for both the A-DRL's and C-A-DRL's actor and critic networks. In our chosen DNN network, each hidden layer consists of 64 neurons and uses a 'tanh' activation function.

6   Dataset and Challenger Detection System

Threat experts identify the threat actor by discovering the modus operandi of the threat vector and the attack surface and correlating these with similar discoveries existing in historical databases. Often to evade quick detection, the malware developer prefers to create metamorphic variants from an older malware repository which preferably is neither public nor available in any recent private databases of the malware defenders; or is otherwise not easy to correlate with. While metamorphism enables the malware to evade detection even from the classifiers trained on their base variants, the lack of recency effect gives the malware developers an opportunity to hide their tracks and avert an expedited discovery of compromise. Therefore, to mimic such a scenario, we use an old. Still, a popular standardized malware dataset named Malicia [16], which has different types of malware samples, viz. ransomware, viruses, etc., belonging to different generations and families; and is also not public anymore (potentially to prevent malware developers from using samples from it to perpetuate any further actual attack). Therefore, this dataset is ideal for the intended purpose. Our data collection, processing, and base classifier training and selection process is illustrated in Fig. 3.

Using this dataset, the A-DRL system attempt to generate malware that could not be detected by a challenger malware detection system which is pre-trained using a dataset that contains its base variants. But to avoid any bias related to the challenger system, we first experiment with multiple challenger systems and identify the best one to embed in the A-DRL/C-A-DRL environments. The challenger system is described and evaluated in Subsect. 6.1.

6.1   Multiple Challenger Malware Detection Systems

We use three series of classifiers, namely the ML, the sequential DL architectures based Deep Neural Networks (DL-DNN), and the recurrent DL architecture based Long-Short-Term-Memory networks (DL-LSTM). With each series, we use compatible and appropriate feature selection/ reduction/ transformation algorithms. From the ML classifier series, we use the Random Forest (RF) classifier, which is one of the most potent classical ML classifiers used for malware detection [31]. With RF, we use variance threshold (VT) as the feature selection/reduction mechanism. For the DL-DNN classifier series, we use the Deep Stacked Auto-Encoders (AE) for dimension reduction [33]. For the DL-LSTM series, besides using feature transformation/reduction using embeddings (AE-based), we need some additional pre-processing to reduce the variation

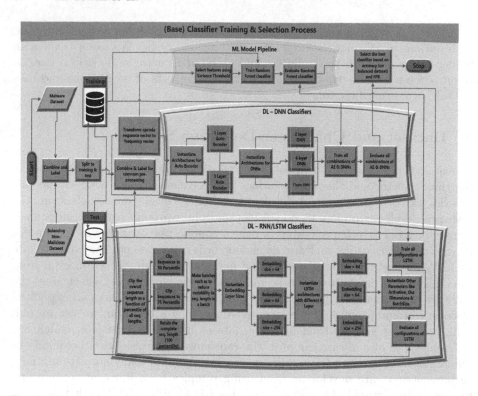

Fig. 3. Flow of the data processing, challenger classifier training, and selection process.

in the sequence length across the samples included in each batch of training. This is essential, as LSTMs are sensitive toward excessive pruning/padding of sequences within a training batch. Next, we train each of the models using (several batches/epochs) of the training dataset. For DL models, the training is stopped on convergence to avoid over-fitting (early stopping). Then, we evaluate the different models on the described metrics using the validation dataset. The performance of the classical RF classifier is given in Table 1. The RF model, with or without the VT augmentation, works well. With VT feature-selection enhancement, the accuracy is slightly better. Also, VT decreases the overall computational complexity of the model due to the reduced size of the feature vector. We chose this configuration for embedding inside the A-DRL and C-A-DRL environment as the challenger malware detection system.

We also experimented with different combinations of the AE, DL-DNN, and DL-LSTM classifiers. The obtained performance is given in the Table 2 and 3. From the considered hyper-parameters and their levels, many combinations of LSTM network configurations are possible. But all configurations did not converge optimally and hence are not reported. Also, some configurations did not lead to superior performance on monotonically varying a given parameter, so these configurations are also not reported.

Table 1. Performance of the classical RF in the pipeline.

Feature	Classification	Acc.	FPR
None	RF	0.994	0.0022
VT	RF	0.995	0.0025

Table 2. Performance of DNN with AE and different layers in the pipeline.

AE Layers	DNN Layers	Acc.	FPR
1	2	0.965	0.0242
1	4	0.977	0.0129
1	7	0.978	0.0165
3	2	0.905	0.0889
3	4	0.928	0.0751
3	7	0.931	0.0897

Table 3. Performance of LSTM classifier in pipelines for the considered hyper-parameters.

No.	Seq.Ln.	Emb.Sz.	No.Lyr	Out.Dim.	Act.	DO	Bt.Sz.	Val.Loss	Acc.
1	100P	64	2	100P	tanh	0.3	32 6	0.7014	0.5625
2	75P	256	2	75P	tanh	0.3	32	0.6933	0.5312
3	75P	256	1	256	sigmoid	0.5	128	0.6989	0.5227
4	75P	128	4	75P	tanh	0.3	64	0.6881	0.5781
5	75P	128	2	75P	tanh	0.3	128	0.6886	0.5625
6	75P	128	2	256	sigmoid	0.5	128	0.7094	0.4218
7	75P	128	1	256	sigmoid	0.5	128	0.7005	0.5111
8	50P	256	1	256	sigmoid	0.5	128 5	0.7082	0.5117
9	50P	128	1	256	sigmoid	0.5	128 4	0.6826	0.5319

Based on these results, we chose the entire malware detection pipeline of the VT-enhanced RF model (along with the feature extraction module). We plugged it into our A-DRL and C-A-DRL training environments to suggest appropriate rewards for the training of the corresponding DRL agent. The added advantage of opting for the VT and ML-RF combination classification pipeline is that both the algorithms are extremely robust to both the adversarial-DL attacks and the gradient attacks and hence could not be fooled by random perturbation insertions. This scenario is ideal for training a DRL agent to favour learning to generate a metamorphic malware instead of trivially adding noise to it to evade detection. Further, we also use additional checks in our system (discussed in Sect. 7 and 8) to ensure that the agents are learning to infuse metamorphism instead of exploiting other tricks even beyond noise insertions.

7   A-DRL Experiments and Result Analysis

We conducted multiple experiments in two phases. In the first phase, we instantiated several A-DRL agents with a custom-designed environment (discussed in Sect. 4). The environment encapsulates the entire malware detection pipeline (Sect. 6.1). The interaction between the A-DRL agent and the environment resulted in augmenting a repository of metamorphic malware/ransomware, as shown in Fig. 2. In each episode, an A-DRL agent is offered to obfuscate and infuse evasive metamorphism into randomly chosen (existing) ransomware. For each of the ransomware offered to the agent to metamorph, the associated classifier pipeline is pre-verified to detect the base variant of the same un-ambiguously as malicious with a probability $\mathbb{P}_{Detection} > 0.95$. Each episode consists of several steps of interaction across multiple episodes between an agent and a randomly instantiated environment. In each episode, the agent was allowed a maximum of 1,500 turns/steps to generate an undetectable metamorphic variant of an existing (base) ransomware.

The experimental results of A-DRL agent training (Fig. 4) show a rising trend in the evasion probability ($\mathbb{P}_{Metamorphism}$) that the agent could achieve, which indicates that the agent is learning a generalized policy to achieve metamorphism. Also, from the results, we observe that in less than 100 episodes, the agent was briefly able to reach the desired threshold of $\mathbb{P}_{Metamorphism} > 0.5$ for the first time. In this instance, the malware classification pipeline started classifying it as non-malicious. Further, at ≈ 150 episode, the agent has learned an effective generalized policy to evade the malware classifier consistently and repeatedly in invariably all subsequent episodes. In addition, we also observe that as the number of episodes progress, the total discounted reward consistently increases. This again indicates that the agent is learning a generalized policy that is applicable for infusing metamorphism in any unseen (not known to the agent) ransomware as well.

The trends of instantaneous and discounted rewards received by this agent.

Often, DRL agents end up learning a trivial trick/exploits to accomplish the rewards instead of learning a desired generalized policy that can be replicated across different scenarios/ransomware. In the context of the A-DRL system, one such trivial exploit could be to transform all ransomware into a standardized feature vector that the agent knows (has learned during training) that will be reported as non-malicious by the classifier. Learning such undesired exploits could defeat the objective of the system because then the evasion cannot be completely attributed to infusion of metamorphism/obfuscations, and such exploits could even modify the file functionality. Therefore, to ensure that the A-DRL learned a generalized and effective policy to infuse metamorphism and not a trivial trick/exploit, we compute the similarity (Pearson Correlation [4]) of the final obfuscated feature vector with the original malware that the environment was instantiated with when the episode began (Fig. 5). A higher similarity indicates that the A-DRL agent has learned to insert minimum junk code(s) in that specific malware so as to enable it to evade the detection successfully, and

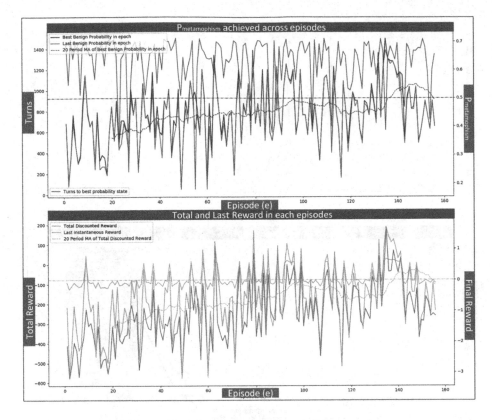

Fig. 4. Training statistics of an A-DRL agent.

the A-DRL agent attained a remarkably elevated level of similarity such that ransomware achieves a decent level of metamorphism.

The feature vectors of the generated metamorphic variant of the ransomware that can successfully evade detection are stored in a repository of the metamorphic ransomware that is shared with the training environment of the C-A-DRL. For each existing (base) ransomware, there could be multiple metamorphic variants of the same as generated by different A-DRL agents using diverse action policies. Also, since these variants are generated using diverse policies (from different agents), such metamorphic variants offer a lot of variety to the C-A-DRL agents to learn a generalized policy of normalizing diverse types of obfuscations and metamorphism. Therefore, next, in the second phase of experiments, we train the C-A-DRL agents using the custom C-A-DRL environment.

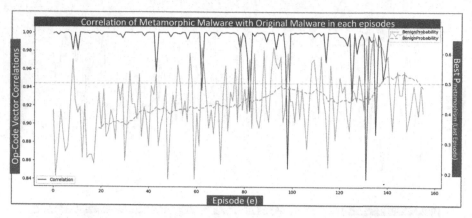

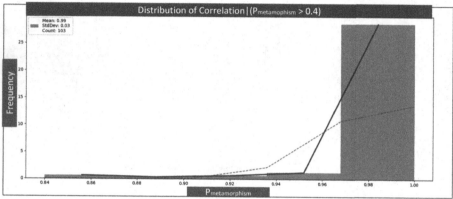

Fig. 5. Similarity trend across the episode and the achieved metamorphism for an A-DRL agent.

8   C-A-DRL Experiments and Analysis

The C-A-DRL agents learn to normalize the obfuscations generated by junk-code insertions from the metamorphic samples generated by A-DRL. Now we intend to train the C-A-DRL agents to learn generalized metamorphism-normalization policy. Therefore, like the experiments with the A-DRL system, we train the C-A-DRL agents over multiple episodes. In each episode, the C-A-DRL agent has been given a randomly selected variant of one of the ransomware to normalize so that it can be subsequently detected by the challenger detection system. Compared to the A-DRL, the C-A-DRL agent took more episodes exponentially to converge. Although the incremental improvement across episodes is slow, it increases monotonically. The experimental analysis shows that the C-A-DRL agent could achieve a detection probability post-metamorphic normalization of $P_{Metamorphism} > 0.6$. Still, it took ≈1000 episodes to improve the $P_{Metamorphism}$ by 0.1 asymptotically.

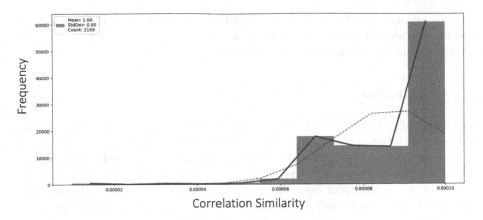

Fig. 6. Similarity of the feature-vector of the normalized ransomware variant generated by the C-A-DRL system with its metamorphic variant generated by the A-DRL system.

Next, we qualify the learning of the C-A-DRL agent through different checks to ensure that it is not leveraging any trivial exploits to attain higher rewards and is genuinely learning a desired generalized metamorphism-normalization policy. With reasoning like that in the case of A-DRL, we can claim that C-A-DRL is also learning a generalized policy for normalization and not just a trivial trick. On a similar line, like that in the case of A-DRL, we can claim that C-A-DRL is also learning a generalized policy for normalization and not just a trivial trick. But just the rising trends in the $P_{Metamorphism}$ for A-DRL and corresponding rising trends in the $P_{Normalization}$ for the C-A-DRL do not guarantee that we have successfully created a malware/ ransomware normalization system. In addition, a ransomware normalization should not only lead to a rise in $P_{Normalization}$ but shall also revert the ransomware to its base variant. So that normalization will ensure that the observed $P_{Normalization}$ is classifier agnostic, and if the malware could be normalized to its original variant form, then any classifier that can detect the base variant can also be able to detect the metamorphic variant post normalization. Therefore, to implement this additional check on the C-A-DRL system, we computed the similarity between the normalized variant (normalized by C-A-DRL) of the metamorphic ransomware and its existing base variant from which A-DRL produced the specific metamorphism. Here also we observe a high degree of similarity (*correlation* ≈ 1.0) which indicates that we have successfully developed a metamorphic malware/ransomware normalization/de-obfuscation system.

Similar to the discussed agent analysis for which we have produced the detailed training and similarity statistics, many more A-DRL and C-A-DRL agents were trained to ensure that we exhaustively cover multiple types of obfuscation and metamorphism strategies and explore effective ways to normalize them. The analysis of the aggregate distribution of $\mathbb{P}_{Normalization}$ has been achieved across different metamorphic ransomware variants, and we find that the system achieved a mean $\mathbb{P}_{Normalization} \approx 0.6$, and for most of the variants the system succeeded in normalizing them enough ($\mathbb{P}_{Normalization} \approx 0.5$) to ensure that they can not evade the existing classifier.

9   Conclusion

We used policy-based A-DRL to successfully create the first-ever metamorphic ransomware using obfuscations at the assembly code level. Next, we trained several such A-DRL agents to create a swarm of such metamorphic ransomware to perpetuate a *zero-day metamorphic swam attack*. The ransomware detection system we used had been shown to be robust against perturbations and gradient-based attacks and hence cannot be evaded using popular adversarial-DL techniques. Next, we also show that our A-DRL system generates metamorphic ransomware by learning a generalized policy to infuse obfuscations in any ransomware and does not exploit any trivial trick/exploit for evasion. Further, we developed a C-A-DRL system as a counter-adversary to our A-DRL system. This system learned to solve the problem of normalizing metamorphic malware at the assembly level. By doing so, the C-A-DRL system was able to normalize metamorphic ransomware to their base variants, which existing detection systems can detect. Moreover, we show that the C-A-DRL successfully enhances the detection probability of the metamorphic ransomware by successfully normalizing its underlying metamorphism and does not rely on trivial exploits for this accomplishment. Also, due to the inherent complexity of the MDP, no popular RL/DRL techniques could provide a feasible solution. Therefore, we used advanced PPO algorithm-based agents that efficiently handle such a large action space and guarantee monotonic improvement.

References

1. Baysa, D., Low, R.M., Stamp, M.: Structural entropy and metamorphic malware. J. Comput. Virol. Hacking Tech. **9**(4), 179–192 (2013)
2. Behera, C.K., Bhaskari, D.L.: Different obfuscation techniques for code protection. Procedia Comput. Sci. **70**, 757–763 (2015)
3. Bilge, L., Dumitraş, T.: Before we knew it: an empirical study of zero-day attacks in the real world. In: ACM Conference on Computer and Communications Security (CCS), pp. 833–844 (2012)
4. Freedman, D., Pisani, R., Purves, R.: Statistics. Norton & Company (1998)
5. Gazet, A.: Comparative analysis of various ransomware virii. J. Comput. Virol. **6**(1), 77–90 (2010)
6. Goodfellow, I., et al.: Generative adversarial networks. Commun. ACM **63**(11), 139–144 (2020)
7. Grosse, K., Papernot, N., Manoharan, P., Backes, M., McDaniel, P.: Adversarial perturbations against deep neural networks for malware classification. arXiv preprint arXiv:1606.04435 (2016)
8. van Hasselt, H., Guez, A., Silver, D.: Deep reinforcement learning with double q-learning. CoRR abs/1509.06461 (2015)

9. Kolosnjaji, B., et al.: Adversarial malware binaries: evading deep learning for malware detection in executables. CoRR abs/1803.04173 (2018)
10. Madry, A., Makelov, A., Schmidt, L., Tsipras, D., Vladu, A.: Towards deep learning models resistant to adversarial attacks. In: International Conference on Learning Representations (ICLR) (2018)
11. Meng, D., Chen, H.: Magnet: a two-pronged defense against adversarial examples. In: ACM SIGSAC Conference on Computer and Communications Security, pp. 135–147 (2017)
12. Mnih, V., et al.: Asynchronous methods for deep reinforcement learning. CoRR abs/1602.01783 (2016)
13. Mnih, V., et al.: Playing Atari with deep reinforcement learning. CoRR abs/1312.5602 (2013)
14. Mnih, V., et al.: Human-level control through deep reinforcement learning. Nature **518**, 529–533 (2015)
15. Mohurle, S., Patil, M.: A brief study of wannacry threat: ransomware attack. Int. J. Adv. Res. Comput. Sci. **8**(5), 1938–1940 (2017)
16. Nappa, A., Rafique, M.Z., Caballero, J.: The MALICIA dataset: identification and analysis of drive-by download operations. Int. J. Inf. Secur. **14**, 15–33 (2015)
17. Papernot, N., McDaniel, P., Jha, S., Fredrikson, M., Celik, Z.B., Swami, A.: The limitations of deep learning in adversarial settings. In: IEEE European Symposium on Security and Privacy (Euro S&P), pp. 372–387 (2016)
18. Rathore, H., Bandwala, T., Sahay, S.K., Sewak, M.: Adversarial robustness of image based Android malware detection models. In: Krishnan, R., Rao, H.R., Sahay, S.K., Samtani, S., Zhao, Z. (eds.) SKM 2021. CCIS, vol. 1549, pp. 3–22. Springer, Cham (2022). https://doi.org/10.1007/978-3-030-97532-6_1
19. Rathore, H., Nikam, P., Sahay, S.K., Sewak, M.: Identification of adversarial Android intents using reinforcement learning. In: International Joint Conference on Neural Networks (IJCNN), pp. 1–8. IEEE (2021)
20. Rathore, H., Samavedhi, A., Sahay, S.K., Sewak, M.: Robust malware detection models: learning from adversarial attacks and defenses. Forensic Sci. Int.: Digit. Invest. **37**, 301183 (2021)
21. Rathore, H., Samavedhi, A., Sahay, S.K., Sewak, M.: Towards adversarially superior malware detection models: an adversary aware proactive approach using adversarial attacks and defenses. Inf. Syst. Front. **25**, 567–587 (2022)
22. Rathore, H., Sasan, A., Sahay, S.K., Sewak, M.: Defending malware detection models against evasion based adversarial attacks. Pattern Recogn. Lett. **164**, 119–125 (2022)
23. Rathore, H., Sharma, S.C., Sahay, S.K., Sewak, M.: Are malware detection classifiers adversarially vulnerable to actor-critic based evasion attacks? EAI Endorsed Trans. Scalable Inf. Syst. **10**(1), e6 (2023)
24. Ren, K., Zheng, T., Qin, Z., Liu, X.: Adversarial attacks and defenses in deep learning. Engineering **6**(3), 346–360 (2020)
25. Schulman, J., Levine, S., Abbeel, P., Jordan, M., Moritz, P.: Trust region policy optimization. In: International Conference on Machine Learning (ICML), pp. 1889–1897. PMLR (2015)
26. Schulman, J., Wolski, F., Dhariwal, P., Radford, A., Klimov, O.: Proximal policy optimization algorithms. CoRR abs/1707.06347 (2017)
27. Sewak, M., Sahay, S.K., Rathore, H.: Value-approximation based deep reinforcement learning techniques: an overview. In: IEEE 5th International Conference on Computing Communication and Automation (ICCCA), pp. 379–384 (2020)

28. Sewak, M.: Deep Q Network (DQN), double DQN, and dueling DQN. In: Sewak, M. (ed.) Deep Reinforcement Learning, pp. 95–108. Springer, Singapore (2019). https://doi.org/10.1007/978-981-13-8285-7_8

29. Sewak, M., Karim, M.R., Pujari, P.: Practical Convolutional Neural Networks: Implement Advanced Deep Learning Models Using Python. Packt Publishing (2018)

30. Sewak, M., Sahay, S.K., Rathore, H.: Policy-approximation based deep reinforcement learning techniques: an overview. In: Joshi, A., Mahmud, M., Ragel, R.G., Thakur, N.V. (eds.) Information and Communication Technology for Competitive Strategies (ICTCS 2020). LNNS, vol. 191, pp. 493–507. Springer, Singapore (2022). https://doi.org/10.1007/978-981-16-0739-4_47

31. Sewak, M., Sahay, S.K., Rathore, H.: Comparison of deep learning and the classical machine learning algorithm for the malware detection. In: 19th IEEE/ACIS SNPD 2018, pp. 293–296. IEEE (2018)

32. Sewak, M., Sahay, S.K., Rathore, H.: Assessment of the relative importance of different hyper-parameters of LSTM for an IDS. In: IEEE Region 10 Conference (TENCON), pp. 414–419. IEEE (2020)

33. Sewak, M., Sahay, S.K., Rathore, H.: An overview of deep learning architecture of deep neural networks and autoencoders. J. Comput. Theor. Nanosci. **17**(1), 182–188 (2020)

34. Sewak, M., Sahay, S.K., Rathore, H.: Adversarialuscator: an adversarial-DRL based obfuscator and metamorphic malware swarm generator. In: International Joint Conference on Neural Networks (IJCNN), pp. 1–9. IEEE (2021)

35. Sewak, M., Sahay, S.K., Rathore, H.: DRLDO: a novel DRL based de-obfuscation system for defence against metamorphic malware. Def. Sci. J. **71**(1), 55–65 (2021)

36. Sewak, M., Sahay, S.K., Rathore, H.: DRo: a data-scarce mechanism to revolutionize the performance of DL-based Security Systems. In: IEEE 46th Conference on Local Computer Networks (LCN), pp. 581–588. IEEE (2021)

37. Sewak, M., Sahay, S.K., Rathore, H.: Deep reinforcement learning for cybersecurity threat detection and protection: a review. In: Krishnan, R., Rao, H.R., Sahay, S.K., Samtani, S., Zhao, Z. (eds.) SKM 2021. CCIS, vol. 1549, pp. 51–72. Springer, Cham (2022). https://doi.org/10.1007/978-3-030-97532-6_4

38. Sutton, R.S., McAllester, D., Singh, S., Mansour, Y.: Policy gradient methods for reinforcement learning with function approximation. In: International Conference on Neural Information Processing Systems, pp. 1057–1063. MIT Press (1999)

39. Usama, M., Asim, M., Latif, S., Qadir, J., Ala-Al-Fuqaha: Generative adversarial networks for launching and thwarting adversarial attacks on network intrusion detection systems. In: 15th International Wireless Communications Mobile Computing Conference (IWCMC), pp. 78–83 (2019)

40. Wang, Z., Schaul, T., Hessel, M., Van Hasselt, H., Lanctot, M., De Freitas, N.: Dueling network architectures for deep reinforcement learning. In: International Conference on International Conference on Machine Learning, pp. 1995–2003 (2016)

Android Malware Detection Based on Static Analysis and Data Mining Techniques: A Systematic Literature Review

Hemant Rathore[✉], Soham Chari, Nishant Verma, Sanjay K. Sahay, and Mohit Sewak

Department of CS and IS, BITS Pilani, K K Birla Goa Campus, Goa, India
{hemantr,h20210029,h20200056,ssahay,p20150023}@goa.bits-pilani.ac.in

Abstract. Android applications are proliferating, which has led to the rise of android malware. Many research studies have proposed various detection frameworks for android malware detection. Literature suggests that static malware detection techniques are practical and assuring for detecting android malware. This paper presents a thorough survey of data mining-based static malware detection. We briefly discuss the growth of android malware and current detection techniques and offer a comprehensive analysis and summary of studies for each data mining-based malware detection phase, such as data acquisition, preprocessing, feature extraction, learning algorithms, and evaluation. Finally, we highlight some challenges and open issues in data mining-based android malware detection. This review will help understand the complete picture of static android malware detection and serve as a basis for malware detection in general.

Keywords: Android · Deep Learning · Machine Learning · Malware Detection · Static Analysis

1 Introduction

Android is the most popular operating system for smartphone devices. As of June 2022, Android owns 71.47% of the market share in mobile OS, with more than 2 billion users worldwide [1]. The Google Play Store, the official app store for Android, consists of 2.65 million applications for download. In addition, Android OS is also gaining popularity for tablet devices and various Internet-of-Things (IoT) devices, such as smart wearables and smart TVs. This ever-growing android market share has compromised android security to some extent.

Android provides various security features, such as the permissions system, to enhance the system's security. However, statistics show that as of March 2020, 482,579 new malware is generated monthly [2]. Due to an open market model, lack of isolation from third-party libraries, and easy-to-reverse-engineer applications, there has been significant growth in android malware. Various methods

W. Wang and J. Wu (Eds.): BROADNETS 2023, LNICST 511, pp. 51–71, 2023.
https://doi.org/10.1007/978-3-031-40467-2_4

have been proposed to enhance the security of the android system, including android malware detection.

Android malware detection can generally be classified into three categories: static, dynamic, and hybrid. Static detection analyzes suspicious android features and does not require running the android application. Dynamic detection performs analysis of the apps by executing them but demands much higher computational resources and time than static analysis. Hybrid detection combines both static and dynamic detection to obtain a balance between detection efficiency and effectiveness. Static analysis achieves high code coverage, and literature suggests it is effective for android malware detection [31].

Some previous studies have discussed static android malware detection. However, there are some limitations in previous analyses. With the emerging novel solutions to tackle android malware, it is necessary to be up-to-date with the current research progress in this field. However, previous studies have discussed now outdated research based on the surveyed literature. In addition, the surveys cover a narrow scope of data mining-based studies, specifically, novel unsupervised learning methods. Data mining-based solutions have proven effective for android malware detection as they can detect new malware, unlike signature-based solutions, which analyze specific patterns with existing known malware. They perform better in efficiency and effectiveness than the previously known approaches. Hence, this study presents a comprehensive survey of data mining-based research to overcome these limitations. The main contributions are:

- We present a thorough and systematic review of data mining-based android malware detection. This paper briefly discusses the background of android applications and malware and focuses on each phase of data mining-based malware detection, such as data acquisition, feature extraction, learning algorithms, and evaluation.
- We extensively discuss the novel unsupervised learning-based, reinforcement learning-based malware detection frameworks and supervised learning solutions to fill some research gaps in previous studies.
- We categorize the proposed solutions and learning algorithms for each section to better understand the advancement in data mining-based research in the field.
- Finally, we discuss new challenges and open issues in data mining-based solutions, such as explainability and IoT solutions, and provide insights for further research.

The rest of this paper is organized as follows. Section 2 describes the evolution of the malware industry, types of malware, and techniques used by malware designers. Section 3 describes the current malware detection techniques and frameworks. Performance metrics used to evaluate the models are discussed in Sect. 4. Section 5 presents the complete data mining-based framework for android malware detection. Previous studies in literature using machine learning and deep learning techniques are discussed in Sects. 6 and 7, respectively. Some open issues and challenges in android malware detection are presented in Sect. 8. Finally, Sect. 9 presents our conclusions.

2   Malware Evolution and Taxonomy

The term *Malware* is derived from *Mal*icious soft*ware*. Malware is a software program designed with malicious intent by the adversary or malware developer. Malicious software enters the computing environment without the user's knowledge and performs undesirable actions like stealing information, corrupting/deleting files, observing behavior like a spy, etc. Malware can be categorized into different types according to its intent and behavior.

2.1   Evolution of Android Malware

Initially, malware developers were focused on computing devices like desktops, laptops, etc. However, as mobile phone technology evolved and the number of mobile phone users increased, many malware developers shifted dynamically to attack mobile phones. Symbian and Windows were the starting mobile OS and were lucrative for malware developers. However, after the evolution and massive adoption of android mobile phones, it became a hotspot for attacks and the malware industry. Android phones gained popularity because of features such as WiFi, 3G, 4G, and 5G, which helped attackers quickly get into the user system. Another motive behind the increasing mobile malware was the growing and flourishing cyber attack industry selling users' private data in the black markets.

2.2   Malware and Its Classification

Malware is a malicious file or program, usually delivered over a network. It is often used to infect, explore, steal, or perform virtually any behavior that an attacker wants to perform against the target. Malware are categorized into different types according to their intent and behavior:

- A **virus** inserts itself in other standalone software programs and is invoked by that program to perform malicious activities or to spread itself [45]. The virus remains inactive until it is activated by the driver program.
- **Worm** is a standalone malicious program that runs independently to perform malicious activities [45]. It needs no driver program to run.
- **Trojan Horse** pretends itself to be a legitimate software program but acts maliciously in the background without user authorization or knowledge [9]. These are hard to recognize, and they attack in the backend.
- **Spyware** is a malicious program that spies on the user or computer system and monitors its activities without the user knowledge or consent [6].
- **Ransomware** installs covertly on a victim's computer and executes a crypto-virology attack that adversely affects it.
- **Bots** is a malicious program that allows the bot-master to remotely control the infected system [46].
- **Hybrid malware** combines two or more other forms of the above malware properties into a new type to achieve more powerful attack functionalities which drastically impact the infected system.

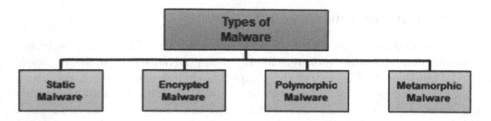

Fig. 1. Types of malware.

2.3   Obfuscation Techniques Used by Malware Designers

Malware can be detected using various malware detection techniques that prevent them from performing malicious activity against the target system. However, creating new malware does not require writing the whole malware code from scratch; instead, various obfuscation techniques can be used to generate many new variants of the same malware with minimum effort. Malware designers can use obfuscation techniques like garbage code insertion, changing control/data flow, package/class/method renaming, string/class encryption, or using reflection APIs. Some of the methods used to create new variants of malware are:

- **Encryption technique** is used to encrypt the malware program so that the signature of the encrypted malware does not match with the signature of the original malware. Identification and decryption of such malware is a challenging task.
- **Polymorphism** includes malware that constantly changes its identifiable features based on a mutation engine that uses various obfuscation techniques to avoid detection, making it challenging to comprehend.
- **Metamorphism** includes body polymorphic malware, as it replicates malware into a new malicious code with minimum to no resemblance to the older version. The mutation engine is also mutated to evade any signature-based detection.

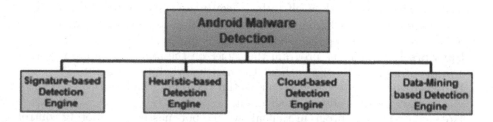

Fig. 2. Android malware detection engines.

3   Current Malware Detection Engines

The anti-malware industry and research community design, develop and deploy various malware detection engines to detect new as well as old malware. These currently include signature, heuristic, and cloud based detection engines.

- **Signature Engine:** All malicious software, programs, and files have a digital footprint/behavior. A signature is a unique string from binary code that identifies a malicious sample/footprint/behavior [47]. If the test file's signature matches the known malware's signature, then the test file is classified as malware otherwise benign.

  Signatures are often manually generated, disseminated, and maintained by domain experts, which are human-driven processes and thus are a bottleneck. The malware designers have also developed tools/techniques that modify a malware sample using obfuscation while maintaining the malicious behavior to generate a new malware variant. The newly created malware variants will be able to evade/fool/bypass the signature-based detection engine, thus making it less effective.

- **Heuristic Engine:** follows a proactive approach where the domain experts design and develop rules/patterns to discriminate malware and benign files/properties/behavior, etc. [47]. The design rules/patterns are generic enough to detect variants of the same malware family. However, rule/pattern generation is again a human driven process and is slow and error-prone.

  Figure 3 shows the design of traditional anti-malware/anti-virus software

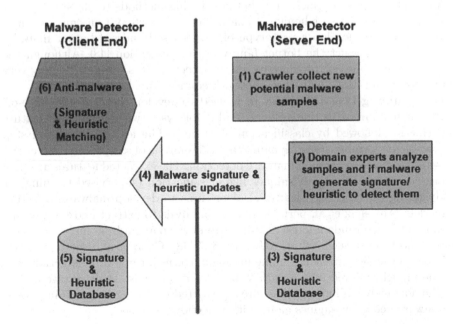

Fig. 3. Design of traditional anti-malware system.

based on signature and heuristic engines. It consists of two parts: malware detector (client end) deployed on smartphone/laptop/desktop etc., and malware detector (server end) deployed on anti-virus company infrastructure. First, crawlers deployed by the anti-virus company scan the internet to find new potential malware samples. Then, domain experts analyze these samples to find new malware samples. Later, signature/heuristic is developed to detect these new malware samples and is stored in the signature & heuristic database. The database is synced from the server end to the client end using regular updates. The anti-virus on the client end executes continuously by taking test samples and generating the signature of the test sample. This signature is compared with the existing malware signature in the database (client side), and if matched, then the test sample is declared malware otherwise benign.

These traditional anti-malware/anti-virus software has two bottlenecks. First, malware signature/heuristic generation is human-driven and cannot cope with the exponential growth in malware numbers seen in the last decade. Second, with the ever-increasing number of malware signatures/heuristics, searching in the database has become slow.

- **Cloud-based Approach:** is a two-layer malware detection strategy comprising a client machine at the first layer and server infrastructure at the second layer. First, the client machine analyzes and verifies the signature/heuristic of the test sample. If found malicious, then the test sample is declared as malware. Otherwise, the test sample is sent to the server for deeper analysis. The server infrastructure has additional malware detection mechanisms from different antivirus engines, and they use voting methods to classify the test sample as malicious or benign. Kedarnath et al. used system calls and network traffic to develop a prototype of cloud-based android botnet malware detection to predict the botnet family of an application [48]. Although the cloud-based approach provides two-layer detection, it is computationally very expensive and needs high-speed network connectivity.

- **Data mining-based Approach:** is used to develop the next-gen state-of-the-art malware detection systems, and it follows a two-step process: feature extraction followed by classification/clustering. The feature extraction step involves performing static/dynamic/hybrid analysis of samples to extract relevant features that help in malware detection. The extracted features are then passed to data mining techniques like classification (supervised learning) or clustering (unsupervised learning) algorithms to develop malware detection models. Abhishek et al. performed static analysis to extract android permissions and used random forest classifiers to develop an android malware detection model that achieved an AUC of 0.817 [48]. Chao et al. used a support-based permission method to mine unique patterns for malware detection [48]. The model achieved 94% accuracy and a very low false positive rate of 5%. The anti-malware industry has already started exploring data mining-based malware detection engines along with traditional engines.

4   Performance Metrics for Data-Mining Based Approach

The data mining-based malware detection models can be developed using various supervised or unsupervised learning algorithms. The performance of these detection models can be measured using the following performance metrics:

4.1   Performance Metrics for Supervised Learning Based Malware Detection Models

Supervised learning algorithms require a dataset that contains samples (malware and benign) and their class labels. The malware detection model is then trained on the labeled data using supervised learning algorithms, and the model is used to perform predictions for unlabelled data in the future.

Supervised learning requires dividing the dataset into two parts-*training set* and *testing set*. The sets must be mutually exclusive to remove any radicalization or biasness in the final results. Algorithms like *hold-out*, *cross-validation* and *bootstrapping* can be used to divide the dataset. For example, the dataset can be divided such that 70% of samples are used for training, and the remaining 30% are used for testing. After dividing the dataset, the malware detection model is trained on *training set* using supervised learning (classification algorithm). The performance of the malware detection model is then evaluated on *test set* using the following performance metrics:

- **True Positive** (TP) is the number of samples that are actually malicious and are also classified as malware by the malware detection model.
- **True Negative** (TN) is the number of samples that are actually benign and are also classified as benign by the malware detection model.
- **False Positive** (FP) is the number of samples that are actually benign but are wrongly classified as malware by the malware detection model.
- **False Negative** (FN) is the number of samples that are actually malicious but are wrongly classified as benign by the malware detection model.
- **Accuracy** is the percentage of samples in the dataset that are correctly classified (malware or benign) by the malware detection model.

$$Accuracy = \frac{TP + TN}{TP + TN + FP + FN} \qquad (1)$$

- **Error Rate** is the percentage of samples in the dataset that are wrongly classified (malware or benign) by the malware detection model.

$$ErrorRate = \frac{FP + FN}{TP + TN + FP + FN} \qquad (2)$$

- **Precision** is the percentage of correctly predicted malware samples over all the samples that are predicted as malicious by the malware detection model.

$$Precision = \frac{TP}{TP + FP} \qquad (3)$$

- **Recall** is the percentage of samples that are correctly predicted as malware by the malware detection model over all the malware samples in the dataset.

$$Recall = \frac{TP}{TP + FN} \tag{4}$$

- **F-score** (F1 score) is the harmonic mean of precision and recall.

$$F1 = 2 \times \frac{Precision \times Recall}{Precision + Recall} \tag{5}$$

- **AUC** is the area under the receiver operating characteristic, and it is used to show the prediction ability of the malware detection model under various discrimination thresholds.

4.2 Performance Metrics for Unsupervised Learning Based Malware Detection Models

Unsupervised learning based malware detection models can be evaluated using *internal* and *external* evaluation metrics. Internal metrics include *Rand index*, *Fowlkes-Mallows scores, Silhouette Coefficient, Calinski-Harabasz Index, Davies-Bouldin Index* etc. Rathore et al. performed clustering for malware detection on the Drebin dataset and used silhouette coefficient, and calinski-harabasz index for determining the quality of clusters [35]. Lou et al. in TFDroid use clustering to first divide android applications into various clusters and then detect malware applications in each cluster [27]. On the other hand *external* evaluation is used when both unsupervised and supervised learning are employed to detect malware. Here, the performance is determined by observing the system's overall improvement with or without unsupervised learning. Rathore et al. developed a malware detection model using a random forest classifier that achieved an AUC of 99.4%. However, when they first performed data clustering followed by a classification model in each cluster, the AUC was boosted to 99.6% [35].

4.3 Other Performance Metrics

The data preprocessing step includes methods to improve the understanding of feature vectors before constructing malware detection models. *Physical* and *Logical distance* can be used to compare different tuples/attributes in the feature vector. Physical distance can be measured using *Euclidean distance, Manhattan Distance, Mahalanobis distance* etc. In contrast, logical distance can be calculated using probabilistic behavior in which past uncertainties are used to calculate future uncertainties. *Pearson correlation coefficient* followed by *Heat Map* can also be employed to understand the relationship between different features or classes. Other correlation metrics includes *Chi-square, Fisher score and Matthews correlation* etc. Shabtai et al. employed chi-square, information gain, and fisher score along with Bayesian Network to construct a malware detection model and achieved the highest accuracy of 92% using information gain [43]. Rathore et al. developed heat maps to understand the correlation between android permissions in malware and benign applications [34].

5   Data Mining-Based Malware Detection Models

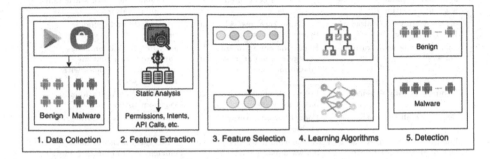

Fig. 4. Framework for developing malware detection system based on data mining techniques.

Figure 4 illustrates the framework for constructing malware detection models based on data mining techniques. The first step is *Data collection* which involves collecting malicious and benign applications for the dataset. The second step is *Feature Extraction*, wherein the application files are reverse-engineered, and features are extracted. The next step is *Feature Selection*, in which the less critical features are removed, and the most relevant features are selected. Further, these features are passed onto the *Learning Algorithm*, wherein a classification model is trained. Additionally, this model is used to classify applications as malware or benign during the testing phase. Each of the steps is discussed in detail in the following sections.

5.1   Data Collection: Android Applications Acquisition

The quality of data (android applications) plays a crucial role while constructing malware detection models. The malware and benign android applications (APKs) in the dataset are generally collected from official app stores such as *Google Play* store and other third party app stores like *apkmirror, apkpure, F-droid, GetJar* etc. Santos et al. collected 13, 189 malicious applications from *VxHeavens* and 13, 000 benign applications from various trusted sources and scanned using *ESET NOD32* antivirus to ensure that the benign applications were safe [48]. Gao et al. used a benign dataset of 49, 000 applications downloaded from *PlayDrone* whereas the malicious applications were obtained from the *Android Malware Genome Project* [11]. Various authors have collected malicious android applications and shared them with the research community like *Drebin* by Arp et al. [4], *Android Malware Dataset* by argus lab [49], *PRAGuard* by University of Cagliari [28], *Kharon* by INRIA [20], etc.

Table 1. Various feature extraction techniques for android applications.

Static Analysis	Dynamic Analysis	Hybrid Analysis
Android application is analysed by parsing its code without executing it	Android application is executed in controlled environment	Android application is analysed using both static and dynamic analysis
Static Features: Permission, Intent, Opcode, etc.	Dynamic Features: API Calls, System Calls etc.	Both static and dynamic features
Scan the code using various parsers	Execution environments: debugger, simulator, emulator, virtual machine	Polyunpack: hidden codes compared with runtime execution + instances with runtime codes
Computationally expensive	Poor performance with trigger based malware	Sometimes computationally very expensive
Better overall code coverage	Poor/Limited coverage problem	Good overall code coverage
Inability due to undecidability, lack of support for runtime packages, limitation to obfuscation	Efficient in analyzing packed malware, more time consuming, requires more resources than static	80:40 ratio makes it more efficient as compared to both the approaches

5.2   Feature Extraction and Representation

Feature Extraction. involves finding features or data patterns that can represent android applications during model development. Features can be extracted using static, dynamic, or hybrid analysis of android applications. *Static analysis* requires parsing the code without executing it. Static analysis of android applications will generate static features like permissions, intent, opcodes, etc. Rathore et al. performed the static analysis of android applications and extracted android permission for malware detection models [34]. On the other hand, *Dynamic analysis* requires executing the code in a controlled environment. Dynamic analysis of android applications will result in dynamic features like system calls, API calls, etc. Fan et al. performed the dynamic analysis and extracted API calls for malware detection. The *hybrid analysis* allows both static as well as dynamic analysis of android applications to extract features. Table 1 illustrates a brief comparison between static, dynamic, and hybrid analysis of android applications. This survey paper extensively focuses on static analysis and static features for android malware detection. Figure 5 shows the percentage of existing papers using a particular static feature for malware detection. Android permission is the most used static feature, followed by API calls and opcode sequences. Other static features include intent, components etc.

Feature Representation. The extracted features comprise raw opcode sequence and *classes.dex* with bytecode. The *classes.dex* contains all the compiled objects used at the run time in the Dalvik environment. These features need to be fed to the classification model in certain representations. These representations are then directly passed to the deep learning models (neural models with n-gram encoding technique) for better classification and characterization. Three different feature representation forms are used: vectorized, tree-based, and graph-based.

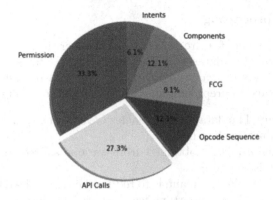

Fig. 5. Distribution of android features for malware detection.

– **Vectorized** representations are the most widely used feature representations in android malware detection and classification. It uses a one-hot encoding technique for vector construction. 'Term Frequency-Inverse Document Frequency' (TF-IDF) and word embedded technique are some of the popular methods. Abhilash et al. used the Doc2Vec technique to create a vectorized representation of a doc file [13]. They obtained a detection accuracy of 95.3% using the LSTM model when trained on 3500 malicious and 2700 benign samples. Karbab et al. proposed the MalDozer framework, which achieved an accuracy of 99.84% [18]. The one-hot encoding technique was used for the vector representation of 33,000 malicious and 33,000 benign applications.
– An abstract syntax tree is formed for android applications' source code in **tree-based** representation. The tree nodes represent the constructs of each source code obtained from the decompression of APK files. Fan et al. used tree-based feature representation for 251 benign and 7000 malicious applications [48]. The decision tree classifier was used with the API calls as the feature set and obtained 95.9% accuracy.
– In **graph-based** representation, android apps are represented using graphs like CFG and IDFG, which help in categorization and are challenging to be attacked by malware. These graphs can be directly fed to the DL models or represented in vectorized form. Jerome et al. used CFG as the feature selection algorithm and created a model with an F-measure score of 0.89 [17]. Gao et al. used CFG for 49,000 benign and 1249 malicious applications [11]. SVM-GFD and SVM-DFD classifiers were used in which SVM-GFD performed better, with an accuracy of 87.85%.

All of these approaches mentioned above are used to improve the performance and efficiency of the models. The ideal feature representation for detection helps in faster training and better accuracy of the classification models.

5.3   Data Pre-processing

Data Preprocessing and feature selection are two critical aspects of machine learning algorithms. The dataset obtained generally contains a lot of inconsistencies, noise, and missing values which makes the data representation skewed. Hence, it is necessary to preprocess the data using the following steps:

- **Data Cleaning:** The data inconsistencies created due to noise are removed, and missing values are handled.
- **Data Integration:** Data obtained from various sources are merged, and redundant data is removed.
- **Data Reduction:** The main aim is to reduce the size of the data by removing irrelevant features. Less important features are identified using the correlation information and removed. Some algorithms used for data reduction are Wavelet transformation, PCA, clustering, and sampling.
- **Data Transformation:** Normalization of data is performed using various techniques. Data with similar functionality are aggregated, and metadata and multi-valued data are handled. Massarelli et al. calculated DFA coefficients for features and given to wrappers for classifier exploitation [32]. Further reduction in the subset is performed after mutual information is collected and passed to the PCA algorithm.

5.4   Feature Selection

Feature selection aims at the identification and elimination of redundant features which have little to no role in the performance improvement of the original model. VetDroid performs analysis on fine-grained android permissions [53]. It proved its usefulness by digging out all the essential syscalls required by the system. They analyzed 1,249 free apps obtained from the Google Play Store. The feature selection process can be done by ranking each feature based on its importance and removing the less critical features or identifying subsets of the most relevant features.

Feature Ranking: Each feature of the set is ranked based on its behavior and importance using pre-existing feature selection algorithms. Some algorithms use mathematical calculations for this determination, while others use rough set theory for the selection process. Using fuzzy rough sets for feature selection has proved its efficiency over rough set theory [16]. Feature grouping was advised to perform better than individual ranking, suggesting that grouped features reduce the time to reach the optimal subset than individual features. Shabtai et al. used 12,075 sample vectors from two devices comprising 1,781 malicious vectors [32]. They suggested that the focus should be on monitoring the malicious processes and permissions rather than the whole system. In addition, they also presented the usage of unsupervised learning over supervised learning to increase malware detection accuracy.

Subset Determination and Verification: Feature selection algorithms are used to identify feature subsets consisting of the most significant features and excluding the least important ones. Tam et al. demonstrated the ensemble feature selection that considers all the feature subsets ranked using different feature selection algorithms [48]. Three significant approaches that are used for feature selection are: filter, wrapper, and embedded.

- **Filter** is the low cost operation focusing on ranking the features based on a score. These rankings are independent of the later stage computation and hold good generalization ability.
- **Wrapper** is a black box technique to determine the best performing subset. It is costly and time consuming. It indentifies different subsets and generates predictions to evaluate the quality of the generated feature subset. The issue of overfitting persists in this approach.
- **Embedded** approach captures the dependencies in a better way and consumes less time than wrappers but is still slower than the filter approach. In addition, it may also suffer from overfitting.

Filter methods are mostly used in malware detection as they are the most scalable and efficient. Some of the examples of filter method include *Document Frequency, Information Gain, Fisherman Selection* and *Maximum Relevance*.

5.5   Different Learning Techniques

Following are various learning approaches that are used to train a malware detector. Each of these methods is suitable for different scenarios.

Supervised Learning: A labeled dataset is used in supervised learning that helps to predict either a discrete variable (classification) or a continuous variable (regression). Liu et al. used supervised learning algorithms like J48 decision tree algorithm and obtained an accuracy of 98.4% [26]. Shabtai et al. extracted 22,000 features, but used 9,898 after data preprocessing using feature selection [43]. They used a top-performing feature set from a group of 50, 100, 200, 300, 500, or 800 features. These datasets were provided to the decision tree and naive bayes algorithm, which gave an accuracy of 90% and 82% with FPR of 0.38 and 0.22, respectively.

Unsupervised Learning: Unsupervised learning is used for unlabeled data where samples are grouped at the time of feature selection and clustering. This approach is quite popular in problems like feature dimension reduction. K. Liu et al. differentiated and mentioned that algorithms like PCA and K-means perform better in unsupervised learning [26]. TFDroid used k-means to cluster data [27]. They tested 2 to 70 data clusters and finalized 32 clusters. They used 5,161 benign applications and 3,247 malicious applications. Results showed that clustering worked better than the non-clustering approach. The clustering approach achieved an accuracy of 90% and a TP of 93.65%, whereas non-clustering gave 84.31% accuracy and a TP of 85.51%.

Semi-supervised Learning: Semi-supervised learning is a combination of supervised and unsupervised learning. Santos et al. proved that mixing supervised and unsupervised performed better. They used the Learning with Local and Global Consistency (LLCG) algorithm with 1,000 malicious and 1,000 benign

Table 2. Malware detection using machine learning algorithms.

Year	Author(s)	Dataset	Performance	Comment(s)
2012	Sarma et al. [37]	121 (M) 1,58,062 (B)	Detection Rate 81% (SVM)	(+) extensive study of amdroid permission (−) malware dataset is too small
2013	Gascon et al. [12]	12,158 (M) 1,35,792 (B)	Detection Rate: 89% (SVM)	(+) can detection local obfuscation (−) expensive (−) evasion possible
2014	Jerome et al. [17]	11,960 (M) 12,905 (B)	F-measure 0.8931 (SVM)	(+) used digital certificate to improve classification performance (−) use only opcode sequence as feature
2014	Chan et al. [8]	175 (M) 621 (B)	Accuracy 86.33% (NB)	(+) used two features (permission & API calls) (−) limited work, small dataset
2016	Fereidooni et al. [10]	Dataset 1: 11,000 (M) 11,000 (B) Dataset 2: 18,766 (M) 11,187 (B)	F1 score Dataset1: 96% (XGB) Dataset2: 97% (XGB)	(+) used many features (+) performed feature selection (−) investigated static features only
2016	Li et al. [25]	388 (M) 322 (B)	AUC 0.8248 (NB)	(+) feature reduction (−) poor performance (−) no comparison with other classifiers
2017	Yanf et al. [50]	640 (B) 640 (M)	Accuracy 95.42% (RF)	(+) use image classification (−) limited dataset
2017	Narayanan et al. [29]	5560 (M) 5000 (B)	Accuracy 89.92% (OL)	(+) use dependency graph with context and sensitive information (−) curse of dimensionality due to many feature
2018	Koli [21]	120 (B) 175 (M)	Accuracy 97.77% (DT)	(+) static and dynamic analysis (−) small dataset
2019	Lou et al. [27]	5560 (M) 5161 (B)	Accuracy 93.7% (k-means)	(+) used clustering for malware detection (+) bag of words as feature (−) curse of dimensionality
2019	Sharma et al. [44]	5531 (M) 4235 (B)	Accuracy 96.32% (RF)	(+) group formation based on dangerous permissions (−) some subgroup has limited samples
2020	Rathore et al. [34]	5,560 (M) 5,721 (B)	Accuracy 94% (RF) AUC 98.1% (RF)	(+) exhaustive study of android permissions (+) used many ML and DL classifiers (−) investigated only one feature
2020	Rathore et al. [35]	5,560 (M) 5,592 (B)	Accuracy 95.7% (RF) AUC 99.4% (RF)	(+) exhaustive feature selection (+) combined clustering and classification (−) only opcode used
2021	Lee et al. [22]	2,500 (M) 5,000 (B)	Accuracy 98.1% (MLP) F1 score 97.1% (MLP)	(+) genetic algorithm-based feature selection (+) used many ML classifiers (−) lower performance than non-selection
2022	Zhang et al. [52]	125 (M) 300 (B)	Accuracy 99.34%	(+) early detection (+) high performance (−) small dataset

applications and achieved an accuracy of 88% on 60% of labeled and 40% of unlabelled data. Xabier et al. also suggested that the model performed better with an accuracy of over 90% with 10% labeled data and 90% unlabeled data, and it depreciated once the amount of labeled data increased [48].

6 Malware Detection Using Machine Learning

Table 2 summarizes various machine learning-based approaches for malware detection. The extensive study of various approaches has led to specific observations, which are highlighted as the advantages and areas of improvement. Fereidooni et al. achieved high accuracy of 97% even though they used unseen malware samples, which imbalanced the dataset during the testing phase [10]. Some works [21,25] achieved good detection accuracy using NB and DT techniques. However, the models were trained on a minimal amount of data. In [29], a combination of dependency graphs is proposed to classify applications as malware or benign. The algorithm using digital certificates proposed in [17] obtained a confidence interval of 99% but is ineffective with advanced obfuscation and growth of feature space dynamically. A novel clustering-based malware detection is proposed in [27]. They investigated 10000 samples and achieved a high detection accuracy of 93.7%. In [37], authors achieved a detection accuracy of 81% with SVM, which used signal trigger function as a metric. However, the dataset was highly imbalanced, with around 158000 benign samples and only 121 malicious samples. This posed a challenge to the efficacy of the model. Rathore et al. combined clustering and classification techniques on the opcodes feature set and obtained the highest accuracy of 94% using Random Forests [35]. Lee et al. performed feature selection using Genetic algorithm and showed that time costs of nine classification algorithms significantly reduced while maintaining good performance [22]. Zhang et al. proposed an early detection framework using system calls and six ML algorithms. They achieved an average early detection accuracy of 99.34%.

7 Malware Detection Using Deep Learning

Similarly, various Deep Learning methods proposed in previous work for malware detection are summarized in table 3. Huang et al. have used one convolution layer with API calls to build neuron matrices [15]. However, the approach followed enabled only offline detection. Lee et al. used the n-gram based RNN and CNN networks for detection which proved to be effective and reliable [23]. Hota et al. used multi-layer data passing technique with doc2vec as a learning algorithm and feature recombination helped in achieving a detection accuracy higher than 95% [13].

Some of the previous research also includes inherent relationship methodologies along with various algorithms of one hot encoding vector, bag of words, and doc2vec learning. Yuan et al. used the Boltzmann machine which uses permissions as the static feature and showed that it performed better than ML

Table 3. Malware detection using deep learning algorithms.

Year	Author(s)	Dataset	Algorithm	Performance
2014	Yuan et al. [51]	250 (M) 250 (B)	Android permission Restricted boltzman machine Deep belief network	Accuracy 96.5%
2016	Hou et al. [14]	2500 (M) 2500 (B)	API calls API call blocks Deep belief network	Accuracy 96.66%
2017	li et al. [24]	5,560 (M) 1,23,453 (B)	Permission API calls and other information Deep neural network	F1 96.08%
2018	Karbab et al. [18]	33,000 (M) 33,000 (B)	API calls one hot encoding Convolutional neural network	F1 96-99% FPR 0.06%–2%
2018	Booz et al. [5]	48,643 (M + B)	Permission Deep neural network	Accuracy 95% F1 93%
2019	Hota and Irolla [13]	Dataset 1: 3500 (M) 2700 (B) Dataset 2: 1,50,000 (M) 1, 50, 000 (B)	Doc2Vec Long short term memory	Accuracy 95.3%
2019	Huang et al. [15]	3,697 (M) 3,312 (B)	API based feature graph Feature selection-Top-20 APIs Convolutional neural network	F1 94.3%
2019	Oak et al. [30]	120,780 (M) 60,390 (B)	Imbalanced data Sequence Modeling Permission BERT and LSTM	F1 score 0.919
2019	Lee et al. [23]	12 lakh (M) 10 lakh (B)	Permission Intent Ngram Convolutional neural network Recurrent neural network	AUC 0.9986
2020	Sewak et al. [38]	5,560 (M) 5,721 (B)	Intent Deep neural network	AUC 0.814 Accuracy 77.2%
2021	Almahmoud et al. [3]	1,430 (M) 1,390 (B)	Permission API Calls System Events Permission Rate Recurrent neural network	Accuracy 98.58%
2021	Cai et al. [7]	7,362 (M) 35,948 (B)	Function embedding Function Call Graph Graph convolutional network	Accuracy 99.81%
2022	Kim et al. [19]	9,000 (M) 9,000 (B)	API call Graph Convolutional neural network	Accuracy 91.27%

models [51]. The DBN outperformed several DL models with a detection accuracy of 96.66%. Li et al. also used API calls and permissions as the feature set with the backpropagation Deep neural network model and achieved a detection accuracy of 97.16% [24]. This model also succeeded in correctly identifying malware families. The dataset contained more than 120000 benign and 5560 malware samples. Almahmoud et al. used permissions, API calls, system events and permission rate as the feature set and proposed a novel RNN architecture that outperformed ML algorithms witn an accuracy of 98.58% [3]. Cai et al. proposed Enhanced Function Call Graphs (E-CFGs) and Graph convolutional networks to generate vectorized representations for app runtime behaviors. Results showed that various ML algorithms performed better with E-CFGs than static features [7]. Kim et al. proposed MAPAS, a CNN-based approach using API call graphs as the feature set. It performed 145.8% faster and consumed less memory than previous state-of-the-art approach and achieved higher accuracy of 91.27% [19].

8   Issues, Challenges and Future Work

Existing literature suggests that data mining-based frameworks for android malware detection have proven effective and efficient. However, some ongoing challenges still need to be addressed. This section discusses open issues and challenges in static android malware detection and provides future research directions.

- **Lack of Representative Datasets:** All android malware detection frameworks require a representative dataset of benign and malware (or malicious) android applications. The dataset collection required collecting android applications from various markets, such as Google Play Store and other third-party markets, and web crawling. This usually led to an unbalanced set of malware and benign applications with very few samples from the malware class. The DREBIN provided a collection of 5560 malware applications from 179 various malware families [4]. However, up-to-date representative datasets covering a wide range of malware categories are necessary to develop data mining-based malware detection frameworks.
- **Incremental Learning** The trained malware detection models must be effective against the repository of known malware as well as newly generated malware. The data mining-based algorithms should also consider the recent malware samples to maintain their effectiveness. The frameworks should dynamically update the training sets to include the new malicious examples while retaining the properties of historical data.
- **Active Learning** Selecting representative samples from a sizeable collection of unknown samples helps improve detection accuracy. Active learning, an effective learning strategy to reduce the cost of acquiring labeled examples and addressing data scarcity problems, has still been used in limited malware detection research. Moscovitch et al. used active learning techniques to showcase the efficiency of the acquisition process and improvement in the

classifier. The framework enabled the selection of representative samples from more than 30,000 files.

– **Adversarial Learning** The rise of data mining-based malware detection techniques has led to malware attackers fooling trained machine learning models using adversarial attacks. These attacks perform perturbations in the training/testing data and force the misclassification of malware samples as benign. Sewak et al. suggested a framework to reduce the impact of adversary attacks in intrusion detection, spam detection, fraud detection, and counter-terrorism [39, 40, 42]. Hence, the detection models must be highly accurate in predicting malicious applications and robust to such attacks [33, 36, 41].

– **Explainability** Data mining-based malware detection models trained on a dataset comprising malicious and benign applications can detect malware in any given application during the testing phase. However, most of these methods cannot justify the decision to classify the application as malware or benign, i.e., the results obtained through primary data mining-based algorithms are not explainable enough. Therefore, the research should focus on the explainability of the models as equally as the performance.

9 Conclusion

The application of data mining-based android malware detection is a significantly developing research topic with many unsolved and unexplored challenges. In this article, we studied the evolution and growth of android malware and the current malware detection techniques and frameworks. We surveyed several data mining-based static malware detection techniques and presented a complete framework for data mining-based android malware detection. Our extensive survey highlights critical observations for each literature and provides insights for further research. Finally, we discuss some research gaps and open issues in this field. We hope this work will boost data mining-based malware detection and inspire researchers to pursue new research avenues.

References

1. Android - Statistics & Facts. https://www.statista.com/topics/876/android/
2. Development of new android malware worldwide. https://www.statista.com/statistics/680705/global-android-malware-volume/
3. Almahmoud, M., Alzu'bi, D., Yaseen, Q.: ReDroidDet: android malware detection based on recurrent neural network. Procedia Comput. Sci. **184**, 841–846 (2021)
4. Arp, D., Spreitzenbarth, M., Hubner, M., Gascon, H., Rieck, K.: DREBIN: effective and explainable detection of android malware in your pocket. In: Network and Distributed System Security Symposium (NDSS), vol. 14, pp. 23–26 (2014)
5. Booz, J., McGiff, J., Hatcher, W.G., Yu, W., Nguyen, J., Lu, C.: Tuning deep learning performance for android malware detection. In: 19th IEEE/ACIS International Conference on Software Engineering, Artificial Intelligence, Networking and Parallel/Distributed Computing (SNPD), pp. 140–145. IEEE (2018)

6. Borders, K., Prakash, A.: Web tap: detecting covert web traffic. In: 11th ACM Conference on Computer and Communications Security (CCS), pp. 110–120 (2004)

7. Cai, M., Jiang, Y., Gao, C., Yuan, W.: Learning features from enhanced function call graphs for android malware detection. Neurocomputing **423**, 301–307 (2021)

8. Chan, P.P., Song, W.K.: Static detection of Android malware by using permissions and API calls. In: International Conference on Machine Learning and Cybernetics, vol. 1, pp. 82–87. IEEE (2014)

9. Craig-Lees, M.: Sense making: trojan horse? Pandora's box? Psychol. Mark. **18**(5), 513–526 (2001)

10. Fereidooni, H., Conti, M., Yao, D., Sperduti, A.: ANASTASIA: ANdroid mAlware detection using STatic analySIs of applications. In: 8th International Conference on New Technologies, Mobility and Security, pp. 1–5. IEEE (2016)

11. Gao, T., Peng, W., Sisodia, D., Saha, T.K., Li, F., Al Hasan, M.: Android malware detection via graphlet sampling. IEEE Trans. Mob. Comput. **18**(12), 2754–2767 (2018)

12. Gascon, H., Yamaguchi, F., Arp, D., Rieck, K.: Structural detection of android malware using embedded call graphs. In: ACM Workshop on Artificial Intelligence and Security, pp. 45–54 (2013)

13. Hota, A., Irolla, P.: Deep neural networks for android malware detection. In: International Conference on Information Systems Security and Privacy (ICISSP), pp. 657–663. IEEE (2019)

14. Hou, S., Saas, A., Ye, Y., Chen, L.: DroidDelver: an android malware detection system using deep belief network based on API call blocks. In: Song, S., Tong, Y. (eds.) WAIM 2016. LNCS, vol. 9998, pp. 54–66. Springer, Cham (2016). https://doi.org/10.1007/978-3-319-47121-1_5

15. Huang, N., Xu, M., Zheng, N., Qiao, T., Choo, K.K.R.: Deep android malware classification with API-based feature graph. In: IEEE TrustCom/BigDataSE, pp. 296–303. IEEE (2019)

16. Jensen, R., Shen, Q.: Semantics-preserving dimensionality reduction: rough and fuzzy-rough-based approaches. IEEE Trans. Knowl. Data Eng. **16**(12), 1457–1471 (2004)

17. Jerome, Q., Allix, K., State, R., Engel, T.: Using opcode-sequences to detect malicious android applications. In: IEEE ICC, pp. 914–919. IEEE (2014)

18. Karbab, E.B., Debbabi, M., Derhab, A., Mouheb, D.: MalDozer: automatic framework for android malware detection using deep learning. Digit. Investig. **24**, S48–S59 (2018)

19. Kim, J., Ban, Y., Ko, E., Cho, H., Yi, J.H.: MAPAS: a practical deep learning-based android malware detection system. Int. J. Inf. Secur. **21**, 1–14 (2022)

20. Kiss, N., Lalande, J.F., Leslous, M., Tong, V.V.T.: Kharon dataset: android malware under a microscope. In: The LASER Workshop 2016, pp. 1–12 (2016)

21. Koli, J.: RanDroid: android malware detection using random machine learning classifiers. In: IEEE ICSESP. pp. 1–6. IEEE (2018)

22. Lee, J., Jang, H., Ha, S., Yoon, Y.: Android malware detection using ml with feature selection based on the genetic algorithm. Mathematics **9**(21), 2813 (2021)

23. Lee, W.Y., Saxe, J., Harang, R.: SeqDroid: obfuscated android malware detection using stacked convolutional and recurrent neural networks. In: Alazab, M., Tang, M.J. (eds.) Deep Learning Applications for Cyber Security. ASTSA, pp. 197–210. Springer, Cham (2019). https://doi.org/10.1007/978-3-030-13057-2_9

24. Li, D., Wang, Z., Xue, Y.: Fine-grained android malware detection based on deep learning. In: IEEE CNS, pp. 1–2. IEEE (2018)

25. Li, X., Liu, J., Huo, Y., Zhang, R., Yao, Y.: An android malware detection method based on AndroidManifest file. In: IEEE CCIS, pp. 239–243. IEEE (2016)
26. Liu, K., Xu, S., Xu, G., Sun, D., Liu, H.: A review of android malware detection approaches based on machine learning. IEEE Access **8**, 124579–124607 (2020)
27. Lou, S., Cheng, S., Huang, J., Jiang, F.: TFDroid: android malware detection by topics and sensitive data flows using machine learning techniques. In: International Conference on Information and Computer Technologies, pp. 30–36. IEEE (2019)
28. Maiorca, D., Ariu, D., Corona, I., Aresu, M., Giacinto, G.: Stealth attacks: an extended insight into the obfuscation effects on android malware. Comput. Secur. **51**, 16–31 (2015)
29. Narayanan, A., Chandramohan, M., Chen, L., Liu, Y.: Context-aware, adaptive, and scalable android malware detection through online learning. IEEE Trans. Emerg. Top. Comput. Intell. **1**(3), 157–175 (2017)
30. Oak, R., Du, M., Yan, D., Takawale, H., Amit, I.: Malware detection on highly imbalanced data through sequence modeling. In: 12th ACM Workshop on Artificial Intelligence and Security, pp. 37–48 (2019)
31. Pan, Y., Ge, X., Fang, C., Fan, Y.: A systematic literature review of android malware detection using static analysis. IEEE Access **8**, 116363–116379 (2020)
32. Rathore, H., Agarwal, S., Sahay, S.K., Sewak, M.: Malware detection using machine learning and deep learning. In: Mondal, A., Gupta, H., Srivastava, J., Reddy, P.K., Somayajulu, D.V.L.N. (eds.) BDA 2018. LNCS, vol. 11297, pp. 402–411. Springer, Cham (2018). https://doi.org/10.1007/978-3-030-04780-1_28
33. Rathore, H., Nikam, P., Sahay, S.K., Sewak, M.: Identification of adversarial android intents using reinforcement learning. In: International Joint Conference on Neural Networks (IJCNN), pp. 1–8. IEEE (2021)
34. Rathore, H., Sahay, S.K., Rajvanshi, R., Sewak, M.: Identification of significant permissions for efficient android malware detection. In: Gao, H., J. Durán Barroso, R., Shanchen, P., Li, R. (eds.) BROADNETS 2020. LNICST, vol. 355, pp. 33–52. Springer, Cham (2021). https://doi.org/10.1007/978-3-030-68737-3_3
35. Rathore, H., Sahay, S.K., Thukral, S., Sewak, M.: Detection of malicious android applications: classical machine learning vs. deep neural network integrated with clustering. In: Gao, H., J. Durán Barroso, R., Shanchen, P., Li, R. (eds.) BROAD-NETS 2020. LNICST, vol. 355, pp. 109–128. Springer, Cham (2021). https://doi.org/10.1007/978-3-030-68737-3_7
36. Rathore, H., Samavedhi, A., Sahay, S.K., Sewak, M.: Robust malware detection models: learning from adversarial attacks and defenses. Forensic Sci. Int.: Digit. Invest. **37**, 301183 (2021)
37. Sarma, B.P., Li, N., Gates, C., Potharaju, R., Nita-Rotaru, C., Molloy, I.: Android permissions: a perspective combining risks and benefits. In: 17th ACM symposium on Access Control Models and Technologies, pp. 13–22 (2012)
38. Sewak, M., Sahay, S.K., Rathore, H.: DeepIntent: implicitintent based android IDS with E2E deep learning architecture. In: IEEE PIMRC, pp. 1–6. IEEE (2020)
39. Sewak, M., Sahay, S.K., Rathore, H.: Value-approximation based deep reinforcement learning techniques: an overview. In: International Conference on Computing Communication and Automation, pp. 379–384. IEEE (2020)
40. Sewak, M., Sahay, S.K., Rathore, H.: Deep reinforcement learning for cybersecurity threat detection and protection: A review. In: Krishnan, R., Rao, H.R., Sahay, S.K., Samtani, S., Zhao, Z. (eds.) SKM 2021. CCISv, vol. 1549, pp. 51–72. Springer, Cham (2021). https://doi.org/10.1007/978-3-030-97532-6_4
41. Sewak, M., Sahay, S.K., Rathore, H.: DRLDO: a novel DRL based de-obfuscation system for defence against metamorphic malware. Def. Sci. J. **71**(1), 55–65 (2021)

42. Sewak, M., Sahay, S.K., Rathore, H.: Policy-approximation based deep reinforce-
    ment learning techniques: an overview. In: Joshi, A., Mahmud, M., Ragel, R.G.,
    Thakur, N.V. (eds.) Information and Communication Technology for Competitive
    Strategies (ICTCS 2020). LNNS, vol. 191, pp. 493–507. Springer, Singapore (2022).
    https://doi.org/10.1007/978-981-16-0739-4_47
43. Shabtai, A., Fledel, Y., Elovici, Y.: Automated static code analysis for classify-
    ing android applications using machine learning. In: International Conference on
    Computational Intelligence and Security, pp. 329–333. IEEE (2010)
44. Sharma, A., Sahay, S.K.: Group-wise classification approach to improve android
    malicious apps detection accuracy. arXiv preprint arXiv:1904.02122 (2019)
45. Spafford, E.H.: The internet worm program: an analysis. ACM SIGCOMM Com-
    put. Commun. Rev. **19**(1), 17–57 (1989)
46. Stinson, E., Mitchell, J.C.: Characterizing bots' remote control behavior. In: M.
    Hämmerli, B., Sommer, R. (eds.) DIMVA 2007. LNCS, vol. 4579, pp. 89–108.
    Springer, Heidelberg (2007). https://doi.org/10.1007/978-3-540-73614-1_6
47. Szor, P.: The Art of Computer Virus Research and Defense. Addison-Wesley Pro-
    fessional (2005)
48. Tan, D.J., Chua, T.W., Thing, V.L.: Securing android: a survey, taxonomy, and
    challenges. ACM Comput. Surv. (CSUR) **47**(4), 1–45 (2015)
49. Wei, F., Li, Y., Roy, S., Ou, X., Zhou, W.: Deep ground truth analysis of current
    android malware. In: Polychronakis, M., Meier, M. (eds.) DIMVA 2017. LNCS,
    vol. 10327, pp. 252–276. Springer, Cham (2017). https://doi.org/10.1007/978-3-
    319-60876-1_12
50. Yang, M., Wen, Q.: Detecting android malware by applying classification tech-
    niques on images patterns. In: IEEE ICCCBDA, pp. 344–347. IEEE (2017)
51. Yuan, Z., Lu, Y., Wang, Z., Xue, Y.: Droid-sec: deep learning in android malware
    detection. In: ACM Conference on SIGCOMM, pp. 371–372 (2014)
52. Zhang, X., Mathur, A., Zhao, L., Rahmat, S., Javaid, A., Yang, X.: An early
    detection of android malware using system calls based machine learning model. In:
    International Conference on Availability, Reliability and Security, pp. 1–9 (2022)
53. Zhang, Y., Yang, M., Yang, Z., Gu, G., Ning, P., Zang, B.: Permission use analysis
    for vetting undesirable behaviors in android apps. IEEE Trans. Inf. Forensics Secur.
    9(11), 1828–1842 (2014)

MalEfficient10%: A Novel Feature Reduction Approach for Android Malware Detection

Hemant Rathore[✉], Ajay Kharat, Rashmi T, Adithya Manickavasakam, Sanjay K. Sahay, and Mohit Sewak

Department of CS and IS, BITS Pilani, K K Birla Goa Campus, Goa, India
{hemantr,h20190011,h20210020,
f20190181,ssahay,p20150023}@goa.bits-pilani.ac.in

Abstract. The Android OS has recently gained immense popularity among smartphone users. It has also attracted many malware developers, leading to countless malicious applications in the ecosystem. Many recent reports suggest that the conventional signature-based malware detection technique fails to protect android smartphones from new and sophisticated malware attacks. Therefore, researchers are exploring machine learning-based malware detection systems that can successfully discriminate between malware and benign applications: *effectively* and *efficiently*. Existing literature suggests that many machine learning-based models use large feature sets for malware detection. However, classification models based on a large number of features are computationally expensive, time-consuming, and have poor generalizability. Therefore, this paper proposes a reliable feature reduction approach to select the most prominent features for effective and efficient malware detection. The proposed approach is tested on two different datasets, three distinct features, and twenty-six unique classifiers. The twenty-six baseline malware detection models based on 724 features and thirteen classification algorithms achieved an average accuracy and average AUC of 94.73% and 94.49%, respectively. Later we performed feature reduction that works with mutually exclusive and merged feature spaces of android permissions, intents, and opcodes. The proposed feature reduction approach reduced the number of features from 724 to 72 (10% of the original features). We also list the reduced set of 72 features comprising android permissions, intent, and opcode used for malware detection. The reduced features based twenty-six malware detection models achieved an average accuracy and average AUC of 93.12% and 92.97%, respectively. The feature reduction leads to less than 2% reduction in average accuracy and AUC. However, it leads to 85.25% and 91.45% reduction in average test and average training time for twenty-six android malware detection models. Therefore, the feature reduction leads to a minute reduction in the effectiveness but results in massively efficient (w.r.t time) malware detection models.

Keywords: Android · Feature Selection · Machine Learning · Malware Detection · Static Analysis

© ICST Institute for Computer Sciences, Social Informatics and Telecommunications Engineering 2023
Published by Springer Nature Switzerland AG 2023. All Rights Reserved
W. Wang and J. Wu (Eds.): BROADNETS 2023, LNICST 511, pp. 72–92, 2023.
https://doi.org/10.1007/978-3-031-40467-2_5

1   Introduction

Smartphones have been an inseparable part of our everyday life and are currently used by more than 50% of the world's population. A recent report by International Data Corporation (IDC) suggests that android holds 72.2% market share of the global mobile phone operating system, and it is expected to reach 80% by the end of 2023 [3]. These smartphones store a large amount of user personal and business data, which is an attractive target for malware developers. Therefore, android smartphones have seen an immense upsurge of malicious applications in the ecosystem. According to AV-Test, more than 33 million malware has been identified in the android ecosystem as of October 2022 [2]. A recent McAfee Mobile Report (2020) reveals that at least 40% of the world's mobile phones are vulnerable to malware attacks, and a new malware is launched every 10 seconds [1]. Therefore, there is an urgent requirement for proactively detecting malware on the android ecosystem.

Currently, conventional malware detection systems are based on signature and heuristic based malware detection techniques [15, 26]. A test application is checked by comparing its signature with known malware signatures in the anti-malware database. To deal with the detection of unknown malware, researchers came up with two broad strategies: (a) static analysis and (b) dynamic analysis. Static analysis dissects and examines applications without executing them. It checks the internal working of the Android Application Package (APK) by reverse engineering. Static features such as Permission (P), Intent (I), and Opcode (O) carry a wealth of information to detect malicious behavior. *Android Permissions* are needed to access critical and sensitive resources [7]. On the other hand, *Android Intents* helps in communication between multiple android components and *Android Opcodes* detail the internal bytecode-level operations of the android OS. Unlike static analysis, dynamic analysis involves running the applications in a sandbox which is a resource-intensive and time-consuming process.

Malware detection based on machine learning consists of two phases: feature extraction and classification [11, 26]. In the *feature extraction* phase, features like Permissions, Intents, and Opcodes are extracted from the android applications. In the *classification* phase, machine learning algorithms are used to construct malware detection models. Arp et al. extracted features like permissions, intents, hardware components, network addresses, app components, and API calls from android applications [4]. They constructed a android malware detection model using support vector machine with a detection rate of 94%. However, they used 545, 000 features and thus suffered from the curse of dimensionality. Li et al. proposed a novel Factorization Machine-based malware detection system using permission, intent, application components, and hardware features. Their approach used 93, 324 features with a resultant accuracy of 99.73% [6].

If the number of features to be analysed is high and the training data is not increased proportionally, the malware detection models tend to overfit. This leads to less-than-expected performance in the real world while also increasing the training and test time. Hence, feature reduction is crucial for static malware detection. This paper proposes a malware detection system that uses limited android permissions, intents, and opcodes (only 10% of the original feature sets) while maintaining high performance. We further combine the original feature sets and find the best 10% features in the merged set. The reduced feature set is evaluated using thirteen malware classifiers from four different categories, and it achieves promising results. We observed that training and testing time reduced drastically after feature reduction. In summary, we made the following contributions with this work:

1. We proposed a novel feature reduction approach for android malware detection, which reduced each feature set to 10% of its original size while maintaining high performance. The number of Permission features were reduced from 195 to 19, Intent features from 273 to 27, Opcode features from 256 to 25, and Total features from 724 to 72.
2. The twenty-six baseline malware detection models without any feature reduction (724 features) achieved an average accuracy of 94.73% and an average AUC of 94.49%. On the other hand, twenty-six baseline malware detection models with feature reduction (72 features) accomplish an average accuracy of 93.12% and an average AUC of 92.97%. The feature reduction from 724 to 72 resulted in a minute average accuracy and AUC reduction of 1.69% and 1.60%, respectively, for twenty-six malware detection models.
3. The feature reduction (from 724 to 72) drastically improved the average training time by 85.26% and the average testing time by 91.45% for twenty-six android malware detection models.

The rest of this paper is structured as follows. Section 2 explains the proposed framework and implementation details of the feature reduction strategy. Section 3 presents the experimental setup and evaluation parameters, while Sect. 4 discusses experimental results. Section 5 highlights related work in the domain of android malware detection, and finally, Sect. 6 concludes the work.

2   Overview and Proposed Framework

This section explains the problem definition and the proposed framework for effective and efficient android malware detection. Later we explain the feature reduction algorithm.

2.1   Problem Definition

Consider an android dataset 'D' containing 'm' android applications.

$$D = \{(x_1, y_1), (x_2, y_2), ..., (x_m, y_m), \forall x \in X, \forall y \in Y\} \tag{1}$$

The malicious applications M are labeled as 1 and the Benign applications B are labeled as 0. X represents the features of android applications and $Y = \{0, 1\}^m$ represents the labels such that

$$y_i = \begin{cases} 1 & \text{if } x_i \in M \\ 0 & \text{if } x_i \in B \end{cases} \quad \text{for i} = 1,2 ... \text{ m, where} |B| \approx |M| \tag{2}$$

Each android application can be represented by features such as permissions (P), intents (I) and opcodes (O). Considering android permissions, intents and opcode features, feature set $X \subseteq \{P, I, O, ...\}$ can be constructed by static analysis of the android applications to train malware detection models. Malware detection models aim to find a hypothesis $f(x_i)$ that reduces the number of instances for which $f(x_i) \neq y_i$. The performance of these models can be evaluated using parameters like detection accuracy, area under curve, false positives, training and testing time. As the number of features in X increases, the training and testing time also increases proportionally, even if only a few of the features contribute substantially to the detection performance. Feature selection aims to find the most discriminating/contributing features to increase the classification models' efficiency and overall performance. The goal is to increase the efficiency of malware detection models using feature reduction, tumbling down the train and test time while maintaining high classification performance.

2.2 Proposed Framework

Figure 1 shows the proposed framework to construct an efficient and effective android malware system. Android applications are collected from Drebin and AMD benchmark android malware datasets. Each set has approximately the same number of benign and malware samples labeled and verified using VirusTotal. Android permissions, intents, and opcodes are extracted from each android application by reverse engineering and transformed into feature vectors for static analysis. Further, we reduce the features from each of P, I, and O independently and in combination using our proposed feature reduction algorithm. Finally, we evaluate the effect of feature reduction on malware detection performance using machine learning and deep learning algorithms.

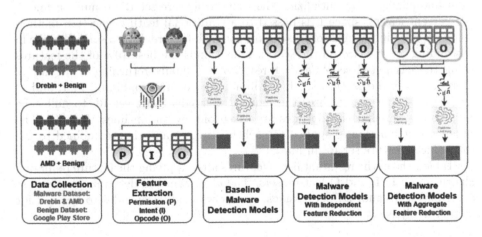

Fig. 1. Proposed framework for effective and efficient android malware detection based on feature reduction.

2.3 Proposed Feature Reduction Approach

Algorithm 1. Proposed Feature Reduction Algorithm

INPUT: Feature Matrix F
OUTPUT: (Reduced set of features, R')
FUNCTION:
getSelection: returns feature importance scores
topFeatures: returns top 10% features
Independent:
1: *Reduced feature set $R' = \emptyset$*
2: *scores $\leftarrow$ getSelection(F)*
3: *sort(scores, descending, inline)*
4: *$R' \leftarrow R' \cup topFeatures(scores)$*
5: *return R'*
6: **Merging**:
7: **INPUT**: $F'_{m \times n} = \{P_{m \times p}, I_{m \times i}, O_{m \times o}\}$, where $n \leq p + i + o$
8: **OUTPUT**: (Reduced set of features, R'')
9: *Reduced feature set $R'' = \emptyset$*
10: **for** each *feature_set $\in F'$* **do**
11:     *$R'' \leftarrow R'' \cup Independent(feature\_set)$*
12: **end for**

Algorithm 1 illustrates the proposed strategy for feature reduction in malware detection models. It consists of two main functions - Independent and Merging. Independent accepts a feature matrix $F \in \{P, I, O\}$ as input, where P, I, O are permission, intent, and opcode vector space, respectively. The algorithm starts from line number 1 by initializing the reduced feature set R' to null. In line 2, the current feature space F is passed to a traditional feature selection method using getSelection, which returns a score for each feature. Line 3 sorts F inline in descending order based on the scores. Line 4 finds the best 10% of the features using the calculated scores and stores it in R', finally returning R' in line 5. Merging takes the feature set F' as input, formed by combining P, I, and O feature sets. Line 7 initializes the reduced merged feature set R" to null. The permissions, intents, and opcodes are taken one by one in lines 10 to 12. The Independent function is applied to each feature set and then combined to get the reduced feature set R" in line 11.

Table 1 shows the resultant list of features after applying the feature reduction algorithm on P, I, and O feature sets. The algorithm has determined the most contributing 19 android permissions, 27 intents, and 25 opcodes to be used for further analysis.

Table 1. Reduced feature list containing Permissions (19), Intents (27) and Opcodes (25).

ANDROID PERMISSION (19)	ANDROID INTENT (27)	ANDROID OPCODE (25)
android.permission. ACCESS_COARSE_LOCATION	android.intent.action. ACTION_SHUTDOWN	OP_CHECK_CAST
android.permission. ACCESS_FINE_LOCATION	android.intent.action. BOOT_COMPLETED	OP_CONST_STRING
android.permission. ACCESS_NETWORK_STATE	android.intent.action. CREATE_SHORTCUT	OP_CONST_16
android.permission. ACCESS_WIFI_STATE	android.intent.action. EDIT	OP_CONST_4
android.permission. CHANGE_WIFI_STATE	android.intent.action. MAIN	OP_GOTO
android.permission. GET_ACCOUNTS	android.intent.action. MEDIA_BAD_REMOVAL	OP_IF_EQZ
android.permission. INTERNET	android.intent.action. MEDIA_NOFS	OP_IF_NEZ
android.permission. READ_EXTERNAL_STORAGE	android.intent.action. MY_PACKAGE_REPLACED	OP_IGET
android.permission. READ_PHONE_STATE	android.intent.action. NEW_OUTGOING_CALL	OP_IGET_OBJECT
android.permission. RECEIVE_BOOT_COMPLETED	android.intent.action. PACKAGE_ADDED	OP_INVOKE_DIRECT
android.permission. RECEIVE_SMS	android.intent.action. PACKAGE_REMOVED	OP_INVOKE_INTERFACE
android.permission. WAKE_LOCK	android.intent.action. PICK	OP_INVOKE_STATIC
android.permission. WRITE_EXTERNAL_STORAGE	android.intent.action. REBOOT	OP_INVOKE_VIRTUAL
android.permission. SYSTEM_ALERT_WINDOW	android.intent.action. SCREEN_ON	OP_IPUT_OBJECT
android.permission. SEND_SMS	android.intent.action. SEND	OP_MOVE_RESULT
android.permission. CALL_PHONE	android.intent.action. TIME_SET	OP_MOVE_ RESULT_OBJECT
android.permission. GET_TASKS	android.intent.action. USER_PRESENT	OP_NEW_INSTANCE
android.permission. READ_SMS	android.intent.action. VIEW	OP_NOP
android.permission. CAMERA	android.intent.category. BROWSABLE	OP_RETURN
	android.intent.category. DEFAULT	OP_RETURN_OBJECT
	android.intent.category. HOME	OP_RETURN_VOID
	android.intent.category. INFO	OP_SGET_BYTE
	android.intent.category. LAUNCHER	OP_SGET_SHORT
	android.intent.category. LEANBACK_LAUNCHER	OP_SPUT_BYTE
	android.intent.category. PREFERENCE	OP_SPUT_SHORT
	android.intent.category. SAMPLE_CODE	
	android.intent.extra. REFERRER_NAME	

3   Experimental Setup

This section first explains the datasets used for experiments, followed by data preprocessing and feature extraction performed in this work. Later we discuss the classification algorithms and performance metrics used in this work.

3.1   Malware and Benign Dataset

The datasets contain malware and benign android applications gathered from various authentic sources. We have conducted all the experiments on two different datasets to validate the generalizability of the proposed approach.

1. **Dataset-1:**
   Malware Applications (Drebin): We have used the Drebin dataset developed by Arp et al., which contains 5, 560 malicious android applications from over 179 malware families [4]. The malicious applications were collected from the Google Play Store, various Chinese marketplaces, and alternative Russian marketplaces. It also contains 1, 260 malicious applications from Android Malware Genome Project. The Drebin dataset is one of the most studied and cited malware datasets available to the research community.
   Benign Applications: We downloaded 8000 android applications from the Google Play store. The downloaded applications were first validated for benignness (i.e., free of malware) using VirusTotal. VirusTotal is owned by Google and aggregates more than 50 antivirus products and online scan engines. Each downloaded application was uploaded to VirusTotal and is labeled benign if all the VirusTotal antiviruses declare it non-malicious. The rest of the non-benign android samples were discarded. The final benign dataset contained 5, 721 android applications.
2. **Dataset-2:**
   Malware Applications (AMD): The second malware dataset used for experiments is the Android Malware Dataset (AMD) proposed by Wei et al. [25]. It contains 24, 650 malicious android applications from 71 malware families that are categorized into 135 varieties. The malicious samples were collected from 2010 to 2016. The AMD dataset is one of the largest android malware datasets available to the community.
   Benign Applications: We afresh downloaded over 25, 000 android applications from the Google Play store between 2015 and 2016. We again used the services of VirusTotal to identify and label benign applications. A downloaded android application was labeled benign if all the applications from VirusTotal declared it as benign. Again, the rest of the non-benign applications were discarded. The final dataset contained 24, 408 benign android applications.

3.2   Feature Extraction

We have performed static analysis of android applications and extracted the key features, namely **Permission (P)**, **Intent (I)**, and **Opcode (O)**, for constructing malware detection models.

The android permission system drives security in the android ecosystem by controlling access to data (such as system data, user data, or system state) and controlling actions (such as accessing the internet, recording audio, or connecting to a paired device). Malicious applications try to fool users into accepting unrelated permissions that can together provide easy access to critical and personal data. They can also perform unauthorized actions on the victim's android devices. This led us to use android permissions as a feature set for constructing malware detection models. We first disassembled benign and malicious android applications in the dataset using Apktool. Apktool is a third-party reverse engineering tool used to assemble, disassemble, and reassemble android applications. The disassembled application contains many files, including the *AndroidManifest.xml* file that contains the application's permission usage. We developed a parser that scanned through *AndroidManifest.xml* of each disassembled application in the dataset and generated a permission feature vector. There are 197 unique system-defined permissions in the android ecosystem. The final permission feature vector is binary, where a row represents an android application, and a column represents the usage of the specific android permission in that application.

Similarly, the android intent system is used by applications to signal to the operating system or other applications that a specific event will take place. It can be used as a messaging object to request specific actions to be performed by other applications. Its functionalities allow communication between components which can result in easy access to highly sensitive services in the android system. The *AndroidManifest.xml* file of a disassembled application also contains the list of android intents used by that application. Our parser scanned the *AndroidManifest.xml* of all disassembled applications in the dataset and generated the intent feature vector. There are 273 unique system-defined intents in the android ecosystem. The final intent feature vector is also binary, where a row represents an android application, and a column represents whether the particular intent is used in the application.

An opcode is the first byte of an instruction that indicates the actual operation performed by the processor. Opcodes can detect malicious attacks at the lowest level of the android platform architecture and are part of the instructions used to communicate with the hardware. Each reverse-engineered android application has Dalvik bytecode instructions containing the opcode and operands of that instruction. There are 256 Dalvik opcodes ranging from 00 to FF in the opcode list provided by android. After reverse-engineering each application from the dataset using Apktool, a parser scans it to generate the frequency of each opcode used by the application.

3.3 Classification Algorithms

We validated our proposed feature reduction technique using thirteen malware classification algorithms in four different categories:

1. **Classical Machine Learning Classifiers**
   Classical machine learning (CML) algorithms are the stepping stones to con-

struct more complex ensemble and neural network-based models. They are intuitive to understand and visualize, lightweight with low resource consumption, and highly interpretable. In our work, we have used the following CML algorithms:

(a) Decision Tree Classifier (DT)

(b) Logistic Regression (LR)

(c) K-Nearest Neighbours (kNN)

2. **Bagging based Classifiers**

Bootstrap Aggregation (Bagging) based classifiers are ensembles of individual CML models. Each model is trained on a random sample taken from the dataset with replacement, thus effectively combating high variance issues. The results are then aggregated to make the final decision by majority voting. The Bagging based classifiers used in our work are as follows:

(a) Random Forest (RF)

(b) Extra Trees Classifier (ET)

(c) Bagged Support Vector Machine (Bag SVM)

3. **Boosting based Classifiers**

Boosting-based classifiers iterate over weak learners, identifying and correcting mistakes while reducing bias until a strong learner is built. Results are generally aggregated by assigning weights to each model based on their classification performance. Boosting algorithms used in our work are as follows:

(a) Gradient Boosting (GB)

(b) Adaptive Boosting (AB)

(c) eXtreme Gradient Boosting (XGB)

(d) Light Gradient Boosting Machine (LGBM)

4. **Deep Neural Network-based Classifiers**

Neural networks are complex mathematical models based on the working of the human brain that identifies patterns and extracts key features in large data samples. It consists of an input layer of simple models/neurons, optional hidden layers that learn more abstract features, and a final output layer. Neurons' output is fed into activation functions that decide the neuron's importance while increasing the level of non-linearity in the network. Deep neural networks have multiple hidden layers to learn complex functions that map the input data to the target output. In our work, we have explored neural networks with different number of hidden layers, as given below:

(a) DNN with 1 hidden layer (DNN1L)

(b) DNN with 3 hidden layer (DNN3L)

(c) DNN with 5 hidden layer (DNN5L)

3.4   Evaluation Parameters

In this study, we evaluated the malware detection models using the following performance metrics:

- **True positive (TP)** denotes the number of malicious applications correctly classified by the model.

- **True negative (TN)** denotes the number of benign applications correctly classified by the model.
- **False positive (FP)** denotes the number of benign applications wrongly classified by the model as malware.
- **False negative (FN)** denotes the number of malware applications wrongly classified by the model as benign.
- **Accuracy** is the ratio of the number of correct predictions made over the total number of predictions.

$$\text{Accuracy} = \frac{TP + TN}{TP + TN + FP + FN} \tag{3}$$

- **Area under Curve (AUC)** shows the performance of a classification model across varying classification thresholds.
- **Training time** is the time taken by the classification model to learn from the training samples.
- **Testing time** is time taken by the model to classify the unknown test samples as malware or benign.

4 Experimental Results

In this section, we begin with a discussion on the baseline performance of thirteen different malware detection models. Detailed performance analysis of the proposed feature reduction algorithms on independent and merged feature sets is presented in the following sections. We also discuss the effect of feature reduction on training and testing time. Finally, we compare the different parameters of our proposed approach with other malware detection systems.

4.1 Performance of P, I and O Based Malware Detection Models

In the proposed framework, we built different malware detection models using machine learning and deep learning classifiers. During the feature extraction phase, we generated three feature sets namely, Android Permissions (P), Intents (I), and Opcodes (O) for the Drebin and AMD datasets. The baseline models are built for P, I and O separately before feature reduction. We trained thirteen different malware detection models based on Classical Machine Learning (DT, LR, kNN), Bagging (RF, ET, Bagged SVC), Boosting (GB, AB, XGB, LGBM), and Deep Neural Networks (DNN-1L, DNN-3L, DNN-5L). The models were trained on 70% and tested on 30% of each dataset.

Table 2. Experimental results based on original P, I, and O (Drebin).

| | Drebin | | | | | |
| | Permission (P) (195) | | Intent (I) (273) | | Opcode (O) (256) | |
	Accuracy	AUC	Accuracy	AUC	Accuracy	AUC
DT	93.58%	93.30%	79.38%	78.80%	93.27%	93.59%
LR	91.52%	91.29%	77.37%	76.93%	88.01%	87.86%
kNN	93.18%	93.08%	67.33%	62.48%	90.63%	90.49%
RF	95.15%	94.99%	79.83%	79.45%	96.01%	96.22%
ET	95.23%	95.18%	80.05%	79.72%	96.04%	96.15%
Bag SVM	94.09%	93.81%	77.50%	76.97%	80.62%	81.94%
ADB	91.37%	91.06%	77.44%	77.29%	92.93%	93.05%
GDB	91.94%	91.63%	78.46%	78.09%	93.88%	94.03%
XGB	94.73%	94.37%	79.80%	79.35%	96.37%	96.76%
LGBM	94.79%	94.61%	79.61%	79.18%	96.23%	96.39%
DNN1L	93.47%	93.43%	78.98%	78.51%	88.02%	88.29%
DNN3L	94.56%	94.51%	79.52%	79.01%	87.07%	87.42%
DNN5L	94.35%	94.30%	80.02%	79.50%	87.01%	87.45%

Table 2 compares the accuracy and AUC of each model for each feature set of the Drebin dataset. Extra Trees Classifiers (ET) performed the best for the 195 permissions and the 273 intents with accuracies of 95.23% and 80.05% respectively, and AUC of 95.18% and 79.72% respectively. For the 256 Opcodes, XGB performed the best with an accuracy and AUC of 96.37% and 96.76% respectively.

Table 3. Experimental results based on original P, I, and O (AMD).

| | AMD | | | | | |
| | Permission (P) (195) | | Intent (I) (273) | | Opcode (O) (256) | |
	Accuracy	AUC	Accuracy	AUC	Accuracy	AUC
DT	94.88%	94.94%	85.59%	85.28%	95.83%	96.08%
LR	93.41%	93.24%	82.63%	82.28%	86.23%	86.39%
kNN	94.90%	94.88%	82.41%	84.54%	94.83%	94.62%
RF	95.97%	95.97%	86.00%	85.70%	97.76%	97.65%
ET	95.95%	95.93%	86.01%	85.74%	97.47%	97.31%
Bag SVM	95.05%	94.69%	83.25%	83.27%	86.86%	87.06%
ADB	92.98%	92.92%	83.34%	82.88%	94.70%	94.62%
GDB	93.50%	93.46%	83.95%	83.69%	95.53%	95.53%
XGB	95.53%	95.57%	85.59%	85.35%	98.33%	98.32%
LGBM	95.22%	95.00%	85.52%	85.13%	97.97%	98.04%
DNN1L	95.18%	95.18%	84.97%	84.84%	92.64%	92.69%
DNN3L	95.34%	95.33%	85.26%	85.13%	89.77%	89.95%
DNN5L	95.48%	95.49%	85.22%	85.08%	87.87%	88.09%

Table 3 compares accuracy and AUC for the models trained on AMD dataset. It is observed that Random Forest (RF) and ET are top performers for permissions and intents, while XGB leads the opcode models. RF performed slightly better than ET for permissions with 95.97% accuracy and 95.97% AUC. ET edges over RF for intents with an accuracy of 86.01% and AUC of 85.74%. XGB performed the best for AMD opcodes, similar to our observations for Drebin, with an accuracy and AUC of 98.33% and 98.32% respectively.

4.2 Performance of (10% of P), (10% of I) and (10% of O) Based Malware Detection Models

A novel feature reduction method was developed over and above classical feature selection approaches to build lightweight and highly accurate malware detectors using the most discriminating/contributing features. Feature scores were estimated for permission, intent, and opcode feature sets in a mutually exclusive manner using local feature selectors. The features were selected until a 10% threshold was reached for the given feature set.

Table 4. Results after feature reduction (10 % of P), (10% of I) & (10% of O)(Drebin).

| | Drebin | | | | | |
| | Permission (19) | | Intent (27) | | Opcode (25) | |
	Accuracy	AUC	Accuracy	AUC	Accuracy	AUC
DT	91.34%	88.46%	78.10%	77.53%	92.05%	92.29%
LR	88.49%	86.11%	75.79%	75.79%	83.33%	83.76%
kNN	90.49%	90.31%	71.78%	61.69%	90.17%	90.32%
RF	92.12%	90.25%	78.49%	78.01%	94.39%	94.44%
ET	91.91%	89.14%	78.66%	78.24%	94.64%	94.79%
Bag SVM	91.95%	89.26%	76.26%	76.02%	79.30%	80.41%
ADB	88.31%	86.11%	75.94%	75.75%	88.98%	88.90%
GDB	89.97%	87.65%	77.02%	76.70%	89.75%	89.96%
XGB	92.20%	89.88%	78.19%	77.68%	94.00%	93.98%
LGBM	92.28%	90.25%	78.18%	77.49%	93.46%	93.50%
DNN1L	91.84%	90.31%	77.24%	76.76%	84.50%	84.95%
DNN3L	91.61%	88.95%	78.48%	77.99%	87.54%	87.73%
DNN5L	91.55%	91.05%	78.51%	78.02%	72.84%	73.96%

Table 4 shows the performance of thirteen malware classifiers after reducing the features to the top ten percent of the original Drebin feature sets (P, I, and O). With just 19 permissions, Light Gradient Boosting Machine(LGBM) achieved the highest accuracy of 92.28%, while kNN and DNN1L achieved the highest AUC of 90.31%. For 27 Intents, ET performed the best, with accuracy and AUC of 78.66% and 78.24%, respectively. The 25 Opcode features achieved the best classification performance for ET with accuracy and AUC of 94.64% and 94.74%, respectively. Comparing Tables 2 and 4, we can see that the performance of the reduced malware classifiers is still close to that of the models trained on the complete feature sets while also reducing the number of features to 10% of the original.

Table 5. Results after feature reduction (10 % of P), (10% of I) & (10% of O) (AMD).

	AMD					
	Permission (19)		Intent (27)		Opcode (25)	
	Accuracy	AUC	Accuracy	AUC	Accuracy	AUC
DT	93.63%	93.57%	85.23%	84.92%	94.35%	94.05%
LR	91.09%	91.06%	81.82%	81.27%	82.61%	82.37%
kNN	93.50%	93.62%	81.86%	84.26%	94.37%	94.14%
RF	94.16%	94.15%	85.55%	85.24%	96.35%	96.29%
ET	94.09%	94.07%	85.50%	85.20%	96.37%	96.39%
Bag SVM	93.71%	93.78%	82.72%	82.76%	86.35%	86.67%
ADB	89.61%	90.03%	82.91%	82.74%	87.71%	88.11%
GDB	92.09%	92.19%	84.11%	83.65%	90.15%	90.18%
XGB	93.97%	94.02%	85.15%	84.82%	95.72%	95.68%
LGBM	93.45%	93.33%	84.97%	84.58%	94.56%	94.30%
DNN1L	93.43%	93.42%	84.69%	84.56%	88.30%	88.46%
DNN3L	93.87%	93.88%	85.01%	84.87%	88.96%	88.96%
DNN5L	93.93%	93.92%	84.83%	84.71%	85.42%	84.04%

Table 5 illustrates the same comparison on the AMD dataset. For the AMD dataset, it was noticed that RF outplayed other algorithms with the highest accuracy and AUC of 94.16% and 94.15%, respectively. For 27 Intents, RF again performs the best with accuracy and AUC of 85.55% and 85.24%, respectively. The 25 opcodes proved to be the best-performing feature set, with the ET achieving accuracy and AUC of 96.37% and 96.39%, respectively. Permissions achieved an average accuracy of 93.12% and average AUC of 93.16%. Intents obtained the least average accuracy and AUC of 84.18% and 84.12%. Opcodes achieved an average accuracy of 90.86% and average AUC of 90.74%. Comparing Tables 3 and 5, we observed that even after reducing the features to 10% of the original feature set, we could maintain the accuracy and AUC close to the original.

4.3   Performance of Merged (P+I+O) and Reduced Merged (10% of (P+I+O)) Based Malware Detection Models

In this section, we compare the performance of the merged feature set (724 features) with the reduced feature set (72) on the malware detection models for Drebin and AMD datasets.

Figure 2 shows that almost all classifier algorithms, noticeably RF, ET, and all the boosting algorithms obtained similar accuracy even after feature reduction to 72 on the Drebin dataset. XGB achieved the highest accuracy before (98.03%) and after feature reduction (97.86%). The average accuracy for Drebin is 92% after feature reduction.

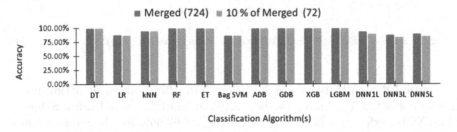

Fig. 2. Accuracy of (P+I+O) and after feature reduction (10% of (P+I+O)) (Drebin).

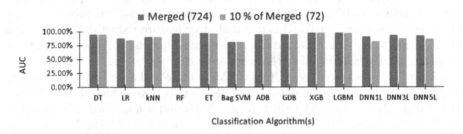

Fig. 3. AUC of (P+I+O) and after feature reduction (10% of (P+I+O)) (Drebin).

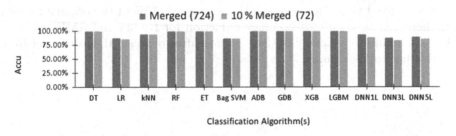

Fig. 4. Accuracy of (P+I+O) and after feature reduction (10% of (P+I+O)) (AMD).

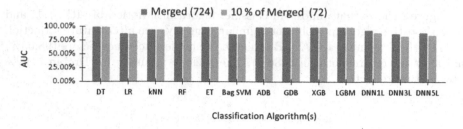

Fig. 5. AUC of (P+I+O) and after feature reduction (10% of (P+I+O)) (AMD).

Figure 3 demonstrates the AUC before and after feature reduction for the Drebin dataset. ET achieved the best AUC of 98.07% before feature reduction, while XGB performed the best with an AUC of 97.65% for the reduced feature sets. All the CML, bagging, and boosting models have achieved approximately equal results before and after feature reduction. The average AUC for Drebin is 91.7% after feature reduction.

Figure 4 demonstrates the near-perfect accuracies for AMD before and after feature reduction. DT, RF, ET, and all the boosting-based algorithms have achieved nearly 100% accuracy for the 724 merged and 72 reduced features. The average accuracy for AMD before and after feature reduction is 95.4% and 94.2%, respectively. It is observed from the results that the 10% selected features are performing almost equal to the original feature set.

Figure 5 demonstrates the AUCs for AMD before and after feature reduction. DT, RF, ET, and all the boosting-based algorithms have achieved nearly 100% AUC for the 724 merged AMD feature sets. This performance was also observed for the 72 features after feature reduction, for which DT, RF, ET, and the boosting algorithms have nearly 100% AUC. kNN obtained the second-highest AUC of 94.7% for the merged set and a close 94.6% for the reduced feature set. The average AUC for AMD before and after feature reduction is 95.4% and 94.2%, respectively. The average accuracies and AUCs before and after feature reduction are greater than 94% for the AMD dataset.

We observed that after reducing the features to 10% of the original merged set, there was only a 1.69% accuracy reduction for Drebin and AMD datasets. The AUC reduced by merely 1.6% on average after reducing the feature set from 724 features to 72 features.

Table 6. Training and Testing time taken by malware detection models on the Merged features and Reduced Features in seconds (Drebin).

	Drebin			
	Merged (P+I+O) (724)		10% of Merged (72)	
	Training Time	Testing Time	Training Time	Testing Time
DT	1.40	0.02	0.30	0.00
LR	3.67	0.03	0.57	0.00
kNN	2.45	5.28	0.19	0.53
RF	1.43	0.08	0.84	0.06
ET	3.21	0.12	0.82	0.07
Bag SVM	148.21	81.29	21.34	7.01
ADB	16.64	1.28	3.22	0.12
GDB	30.93	0.05	6.80	0.01
XGB	18.24	0.14	2.38	0.02
LGBM	6.95	0.15	0.56	0.02
DNN1L	229.89	96.43	21.77	4.52
DNN3L	242.52	125.21	23.95	4.50
DNN5L	454.89	352.46	29.30	5.56

Table 7. Training and Testing time taken by malware detection models on the Merged features and Reduced Features in seconds (AMD).

	AMD			
	Merged (P+I+O) (724)		10% of Merged (72)	
	Training Time	Testing Time	Training Time	Testing Time
DT	0.86	0.06	0.41	0.01
LR	14.76	0.22	7.96	0.01
kNN	14.07	46.42	1.10	6.89
RF	7.25	0.20	2.45	0.08
ET	8.93	0.48	1.65	0.15
Bag SVM	2,862.31	1,014.27	435.40	109.50
ADB	60.58	3.60	15.73	0.58
GDB	106.57	0.23	31.66	0.05
XGB	28.22	0.30	4.70	0.04
LGBM	5.92	0.27	1.12	0.05
DNN1L	528.33	196.22	73.06	20.00
DNN3L	519.96	198.17	82.31	19.20
DNN5L	562.08	196.05	97.33	19.27

4.4   Effect of Feature Reduction on Training Time and Testing Time

With an increase in dimensionality, there is a proportional increase in space, time, and resource consumption, especially when we merge all the feature spaces. However, some features contribute more to the model's discrimination capability than others. In our study, we observed that if only the most contributing features are used to train the models, their performance is similar to the original feature set and their training and testing time reduces drastically. Drebin's highest reduction in training time was 93% with DNN5L, and the lowest was 41% with RF. The highest reduction in testing time was nearly 100% for DT and LR, followed by DNN5L with 98%, and the lowest was 25% with RF.

Similarly, for AMD, kNN achieved the highest reduction in training time with 92.18% and the least was for LR with 46%. LR, DNN1L, and Bag-SVM reduced their testing time by 95%, 89.8%, and 89.2% for AMD, while the least test time reduction was 60% by RF. It is worth noting that the feature reduction creates a tumbling effect on training and testing time. After the proposed feature reduction, the testing time improved drastically by 91.45% on average for the Drebin and AMD datasets. Likewise, the training time improved by 85.25% on average after the feature reduction. The experimental results prove that if the top contributing features are selected for malware detection, there is almost no loss in detection performance, while the training and testing time is reduced drastically. Our proposed algorithm reduced features to the top 10% of the feature sets to build efficient and effective malware detection models.

Table 8. Comparison with existing literature in android malware detection.

Authors	Original Number of Features	Feature Selection	Reduced Number of Features	Feature List	Number and Classifier Used	Detection Accuracy
Arp et al. [4]	545,000	No	-	Yes	1: Linear SVM	94%
C.Li et al. [6]	294,019	No	-	No	1: Factorization Machine	99%
Tangil et al. [22]	20,000	Yes	1000	Yes	1: ET	99.82%
Latha et al. [10]	4115	Yes	518	No	5:RF, SVM, kNN,DT, NC	93.73%
McLaughlin et al. [9]	218	No	-	No	CNN	98%
Wang et al. [23]	135	Yes	40	Yes	3:SVM,DT, RF	94.62%
Chen et al. [5]	230	Yes	107	No	4: RF, SVM,kNN, NB	N/A
Wang et al. [24]	112	Yes	70	Yes	4:NB, DT,NN, kNN	94 - 98%
Our Proposed System	724	Yes	72	Yes	13:CML, Bagging,Boosting,DNN	99.99%

4.5   Comparative Analysis with Existing Literature

Table 8 compares our experimental results with existing literature in the domain of malware detection. Feature reduction is a critical step to avoid the curse of dimensionality, especially in static analysis-based malware detection. Arp et al. used a massive set of 545,000 features and achieved a detection accuracy of

94% [4]. Similarly, Li et al. have also used an entire set of 294, 019 permissions and intents to achieve an accuracy of 99.73% for Drebin and 99.05% for AMD [5]. These approaches have failed to find a balance between detection effectiveness and efficiency. [10, 22] and [5] have performed feature selection and reduced their feature sets to 1000, 518, and 107 features. They evaluated their approaches on only 1, 5, and 4 machine learning models, respectively, while we have systematically evaluated our proposed system on 13 classifiers from 4 different categories. Despite using fewer features, our proposed system achieved higher detection performance. Wang et al. analyzed android permissions and selected 40 risky permissions [23]. Using permission-based features alone can cause the model to miss significant malicious behavior that could have been noticed if opcodes and intents were also considered. Wang et al. performed dynamic analysis and extracted 112 kernel features, which were further reduced to 70 [24]. However, their approach is highly resource-intensive, with large memory consumption, data collection, and training costs. In contrast, we improved our training time by 93.55% and testing time by 98.42%.

5   Related Work

Android malware has been a serious concern in recent years [12, 14, 19]. The anti-malware research community and the security industry are actively working on improving malware detection systems while balancing their effectiveness, computational complexity, resource usage, and training and testing time [18, 20, 21]. Most studies use a single feature space over the same dataset to build malware prediction models using machine learning [13, 16, 17]. According to a study conducted by Liu et al. between 2014 and 2020, 68 out of 132 papers on android malware defenses were based on permissions [8]. Sun et al. extracted 22 significant permissions out of 135 by performing 3-level pruning on the android permissions features set, achieving 90% accuracy [22]. Wen et al. proposed the PCA-RELIEF feature selection algorithm to find discriminative feature subgroups [22]. They obtained an accuracy of 95.2% using SVM trained on Drebin permissions. However, the work lacks validation from a variety of feature spaces and datasets. Chen et al. trained on opcode sequences alone, achieving a detection rate/TPR of 98.8% [5]. They assigned ten symbols to each type of instruction and used the symbol sequences to train their models. Latha et al. proposed the BOAWFS feature selection method based on Bat optimization to reduce the number of permission features in the CICInvesAndMal2019 android malware dataset [10]. They reduced 4115 features to 518 features and achieved a detection accuracy of 93.73%. However, flagging an application as malware or benign based only on knowledge gained from a single feature type can result in missing out on the overall picture. DroidSeive used syntactic and resource-centric features that hinted at malware obfuscation [22]. Around 1000 features were selected out of 20000 and trained using the Extra trees classifier, achieving a detection accuracy of 99.82%. Their work was not validated with a variety of machine-learning algorithms.

Most of the research works have categorized an application as malware or safe based on a single feature space like permissions or opcodes. The trained models would be more ignorant than models trained on a variety of features. The community has focused on improving detection performance at the cost of efficiency by using large feature sets. This is counter-intuitive as large feature sets can lead to overfitting and the curse of dimensionality, thus reducing the models' real-world performance. It also increases resource consumption, training time, and evaluation time. Studies that have performed feature reduction have not validated their approach and feature set using a variety of machine learning-based malware detection models. The selected features were also not published for further validation.

6 Conclusion

Android OS is synonymous with smartphones these days. Its wide usage, global market share, and ease of application development led to android platforms becoming a breeding ground for malware applications. Current signature-based malware detectors identify malware by comparing with known malware signature databases, but they cannot detect unknown malware. This resulted in a shift to machine learning-based malware detectors. Since android applications produce high dimensional data for machine learning, it is crucial to apply feature reduction techniques to reduce computational time and cost. In this paper, we proposed a feature reduction strategy for static analysis-based malware detection systems. To test the viability of our proposed work, we used two different Android malware data sources, namely Drebin and AMD datasets, to build a total of twenty-six models based on thirteen machine learning algorithms in four different categories (Classical ML, Bagging, Boosting, and DNN). Initially, we built baseline models on the individual permissions (195), intents (273), and opcode (256) feature sets, and then merged the feature sets to 724 features. The proposed feature reduction technique reduced each feature set to 10% of its original dimensions (i.e.) 195 permissions were reduced to 19 features, 273 Intents to 27 features, 256 Opcodes to 25 features, and the merged features (724) to just 72 features. We obtained an average accuracy of 94.73% before feature reduction on the merged features and 93.12% after feature reduction, resulting in just 1.69% reduction. Merged features before reduction achieved an AUC of 94.49% while the reduced features achieved 92.97% resulting in a mere 1.61% reduction. We reduced the average training time drastically by 85.26% and the average testing time by 91.45%. The proposed feature reduction approach resulted in huge reduction in training and testing time while achieving high detection performance comparable to the original high dimensional feature set. In the future, we will focus on adversarial attack and defense strategies to make our malware detection systems more robust against adversarial attacks.

References

1. McAfee Mobile Threat Report. https://www.mcafee.com/en-us/consumer-support/2020-mobile-threat-report.html (2020). Accessed Jan 2023
2. AVTEST. https://portal.av-atlas.org/malware/statistics (2022). Accessed Jan 2023
3. IDC Smartphone Market Share. https://www.idc.com/promo/smartphone-market-share (2022). Accessed Jan 2023
4. Arp, D., Spreitzenbarth, M., Hubner, M., Gascon, H., Rieck, K.: Drebin: effective and explainable detection of android malware in your pocket. In: Network and Distributed System Security (NDSS) Symposium, vol. 14, pp. 23–26 (2014)
5. Chen, T., Mao, Q., Yang, Y., Zhu, J.: TinyDroid: a lightweight and efficient model for android malware detection & classification. Mobile Inf. Syst. **2018**, 1–9 (2018)
6. Li, C., Mills, K., Niu, D., Zhu, R., Zhang, H., Kinawi, H.: Android malware detection based on factorization machine. IEEE Access **7**, 184008–184019 (2019)
7. Li, J., Sun, L., Yan, Q., Li, Z., Srisa-An, W., Ye, H.: Significant permission identification for machine-learning-based android malware detection. IEEE Trans. Industr. Inf. **14**(7), 3216–3225 (2018)
8. Liu, Y., Tantithamthavorn, C., Li, L., Liu, Y.: Deep learning for android malware defenses: a systematic literature review. arXiv preprint arXiv:2103.05292 (2021)
9. McLaughlin, N., et al.: Deep android malware detection. In: ACM Conference On Data and Application Security and PrivacY (CODASPY), pp. 301–308 (2017)
10. Pushpa Latha, D.: Bat optimization algorithm for wrapper-based feature selection and performance improvement of android malware detection (2021)
11. Qiu, J., Zhang, J., Luo, W., Pan, L., Nepal, S., Xiang, Y.: A survey of android malware detection with deep neural models. ACM Comput. Surv. (CSUR) **53**(6), 1–36 (2020)
12. Rathore, H., Nikam, P., Sahay, S.K., Sewak, M.: Identification of adversarial android intents using reinforcement learning. In: International Joint Conference on Neural Networks (IJCNN), pp. 1–8. IEEE (2021)
13. Rathore, H., Sahay, S.K., Thukral, S., Sewak, M.: Detection of malicious android applications: classical machine learning vs. deep neural network integrated with clustering. In: Gao, H., J. Durán Barroso, R., Shanchen, P., Li, R. (eds.) BROADNETS 2020. LNICST, vol. 355, pp. 109–128. Springer, Cham (2021). https://doi.org/10.1007/978-3-030-68737-3_7
14. Rathore, H., Samavedhi, A., Sahay, S.K., Sewak, M.: Robust malware detection models: learning from adversarial attacks and defenses. Foren. Sci. Int. Digit. Investig. **37**, 301183 (2021)
15. Sewak, M., Sahay, S.K., Rathore, H.: An investigation of a deep learning based malware detection system. In: 13th International Conference on Availability, Reliability and Security (ARES), pp. 1–5 (2018)
16. Sewak, M., Sahay, S.K., Rathore, H.: Assessment of the relative importance of different hyper-parameters of LSTM for an IDS. In: IEEE Region 10 Conference (TENCON), pp. 414–419. IEEE (2020)
17. Sewak, M., Sahay, S.K., Rathore, H.: DeepIntent: implicitintent based android IDS with E2E deep learning architecture. In: International Symposium on Personal, Indoor and Mobile Radio Communications (PIMRC), pp. 1–6. IEEE (2020)
18. Sewak, M., Sahay, S.K., Rathore, H.: Value-approximation based deep reinforcement learning techniques: an overview. In: International Conference on Computing Communication and Automation, pp. 379–384. IEEE (2020)

19. Sewak, M., Sahay, S.K., Rathore, H.: Deep reinforcement learning for cybersecurity threat detection and protection: a review. In: Krishnan, R., Rao, H.R., Sahay, S.K., Samtani, S., Zhao, Z. (eds.) Secure Knowledge Management In The Artificial Intelligence Era. SKM 2021. Communications in Computer and Information Science, vol. 1549, pp. 51–72. Springer, Cham (2021). https://doi.org/10.1007/978-3-030-97532-6_4

20. Sewak, M., Sahay, S.K., Rathore, H.: DRLDO: a novel DRL based de-obfuscation system for defence against metamorphic malware. Def. Sci. J. **71**(1), 55–65 (2021)

21. Sewak, M., Sahay, S.K., Rathore, H.: DRo: a data-scarce mechanism to revolutionize the performance of DL-based security systems. In: IEEE 46th Conference on Local Computer Networks (LCN), pp. 581–588. IEEE (2021)

22. Sun, L., Li, Z., Yan, Q., Srisa-an, W., Pan, Y.: SigPID: significant permission identification for android malware detection. In: 11th International Conference on Malicious and unwanted software (MALWARE), pp. 1–8. IEEE (2016)

23. Wang, W., Wang, X., Feng, D., Liu, J., Han, Z., Zhang, X.: Exploring permission-induced risk in android applications for malicious application detection. IEEE Trans. Inf. Forensics Secur. **9**(11), 1869–1882 (2014)

24. Wang, X., Li, C.: Android malware detection through machine learning on kernel task structures. Neurocomputing **435**, 126–150 (2021)

25. Wei, F., Li, Y., Roy, S., Ou, X., Zhou, W.: Deep ground truth analysis of current android malware. In: Polychronakis, M., Meier, M. (eds.) DIMVA 2017. LNCS, vol. 10327, pp. 252–276. Springer, Cham (2017). https://doi.org/10.1007/978-3-319-60876-1_12

26. Ye, Y., Li, T., Adjeroh, D., Iyengar, S.S.: A survey on malware detection using data mining techniques. ACM Comput. Surv. (CSUR) **50**(3), 1–40 (2017)

Algorithm, Model and Application

BCTM: A Topic Modeling Method Based on External Information

Gang Liu[1,3], Taiying Wan[1,3(✉)], Jinfeng Yu[1,3], Kai Zhan[2], and Wei Wang[1,3]

[1] College of Computer Science and Technology, Harbin Engineering University,
Harbin 150001, China
wantaiying@hrbeu.edu.cn
[2] PwC Enterprise Digital, PricewaterhouseCoopers, Sydney, NSW 2070, Australia
[3] National Engineering Laboratory of E-Government Modeling Simulation,
Harbin Engineering University, Harbin 150001, China

Abstract. Topic models are often used as intermediate algorithms for text mining and semantic analysis in natural language processing, and have a wide range of functions. However, most of the existing improvements to the topic model use word embedding to improve the accuracy of text modeling, but ignore the external information in the text. This paper proposes a topic model BCTM (Bi-Concept Topic Model) using the word feature information and concept information. Based on the BTM topic model, BCTM introduces word feature information through word vector technology and concept information based on ConceptNet to optimize topic modeling. The construction method of Bi-Concept pair is proposed. Based on ConceptNet semantic network, and the content of text is enriched with concept information. A more accurate topic distribution is obtained through the improved topic model, at the same time, due to the rich feature information, the model is also superior to the baseline model in short text modeling. The experiments prove that the bilingual topic model proposed in this paper has a good performance in modeling accuracy.

Keywords: Topic modeling · Word embedding · External information

1 Introduction

The study of natural language is no longer limited to linguistics, history and other liberal arts fields, the use of computers to deal with natural language is an important development direction of artificial intelligence [1]. With the rapid development of the Internet, a large number of text data are generated in social networks, online shopping, news sites and other information flow sites, which are difficult to find in traditional information sources, so there is a demand for unsupervised topic analysis. Probability-based topic models such as LDA [2] are common methods for this task. Topic models are widely used and are often used to extract various text features [3].

© ICST Institute for Computer Sciences, Social Informatics and Telecommunications Engineering 2023
Published by Springer Nature Switzerland AG 2023. All Rights Reserved
W. Wang and J. Wu (Eds.): BROADNETS 2023, LNICST 511, pp. 95–110, 2023.
https://doi.org/10.1007/978-3-031-40467-2_6

In recent years, improving the topic model and making it suitable for short text mining has become a hot research direction in the field. Some researchers improve the modeling quality of short text by expanding text information, such as aggregating short text into pseudo-documents and extracting features by topic modeling based on pseudo-document expectations. Some scholars assume that the number of topics in the short text is sparse and the document is constrained in a small number of topics, but this method is not suitable for situations where the short text may cover multiple topics. But intuitively, because the aggregation of pseudo-documents will inevitably bring noise, it is difficult to ensure the quality of topics based on pseudo-documents, so it is necessary to take other ways to deal with "noise reduction".

External information is a good way to enrich text information. The external information in this paper is embodied in conceptual information and word feature information. Word vector techniques such as Glove [4] can bring great help to topic semantic enhancement, because the pre-trained word vector model can well supplement the sparse features of short texts. In addition to the frequently used word vectors, external information such as author tags and timestamps of the text can theoretically be used to improve the quality of short text modeling.

In summary, this paper proposes an optimized BTM improved model BCTM,. The main contributions are as follows:

The model overcomes the shortcomings of the previously mentioned model, such as complex structure, non-conjugation and single channel of information acquisition, by transforming meta-information into word label information. The tag information is independent of the model itself so that words with similar tags have similar distribution weights on the topic.

This paper puts forward the construction method of Bi-Concept pair, which enriches the content of the text by introducing conceptual information, so as to construct an effective topic model on the short text.

Several groups of experiments were carried out with confusion degree and theme consistency as evaluation indexes. Experiments show that compared with LDA and other models, the BCTM model based on external information performs better under the same conditions.

2   Related Work

2.1   Topic Model

Since David Blei and others put forward the classical probabilistic topic model LDA, scholars in the field have strong interest and enthusiasm on how to improve this model. LDA belongs to a three-layer Bayesian network structure and has good scalability. Because LDA belongs to the word bag model, it does not consider the order of words and context, which provides a lot of room for the improvement of LDA [5].

The traditional LDA topic model does not perform well in short texts, but its defect is that it does not have enough lexical information to make its statistical meaning valid. How to enrich document information and apply it to short text topic modeling is one of the hot research directions of scholars in recent years.

Document aggregation is an idea of information expansion based on the original text. Zhao [6] proposed a generation model, which aggregates short texts into clusters by using relevant meta-information, which alleviates the poor modeling effect of LDA in short texts. From the point of view of words, Yan [7] proposed a topic model BTM (Biterm Topic Model), which constructs short texts as two-word (biterm) sets. The model makes up for the text sparsity of short texts, and its sampling is based on biterm pairs, which enhances the word co-occurrence of short texts at the document level. In recent years, researchers have made an endless stream of studies on the improvement of classical models. For example, Wu [8], Zhu [9], Li [10] and Huang [11] have made improvements based on the BTM model, but the short text aggregates long text at the same time can not avoid noise, the accuracy of this method is difficult to be effectively guaranteed.

The general idea of introducing word vector feature is to increase the accuracy of topic-word distribution by making words with similar semantics more likely to be assigned to the same topic. Nguyen [12] proposed a LF-LDA (Latent-Feature LDA) model, which combines the word vectors trained by the external corpus into the topic modeling, and extends the topic model to change the Dirichlet component at the topic-word level into a mixture of the word vector and the original subject word distribution. Li [13] proposed the GPU-PDMM model. In the sampling process, the generalized P ó lya urn (GPU) model is used to promote the semantic related words under the same topic, and through the GPU model, the background knowledge about the semantic relations of words learned from millions of external documents can be easily used to improve the topic modeling of short text. Gao [14] proposed the CRFTM (Conditional Random Field regularized Topic Model) model, which uses a conditional random field regularization model so that related words can share the same topic assignment. At the same time, such methods only rely on word vectors to enrich word co-occurrence information, while other external information such as conceptual information between words are not effectively used, so although the accuracy of the model is higher than that of LDA model, there is still room for improvement.

2.2 External Information

The existing improved topic models often ignore the rich external information in the corpus, which also provides a new direction for the research of topic modeling in this paper. External information refers to the information outside the content of the text. Compared with the independent text, the word feature information of the text vocabulary, the associated knowledge information, the label of the text label and so on belong to the external information. The introduction of external information increases the access to information, which can effectively improve the accuracy of modeling.

3 BCTM Model Based on External Information

3.1 Overview of the Model

On the basis of the BTM model, the BCTM model proposed in this paper mainly constructs the short text topic model from the following points, and the specific probability model is shown in Fig. 1.

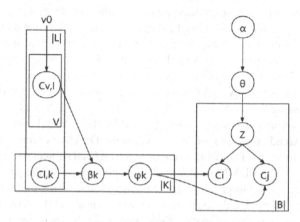

Fig. 1. BCTM probability model diagram

The main contents are as follows:

(1) the word feature information is introduced by the way of label. Lexical features are introduced as external information as a priori in order to make words with similar features have similar Dirichlet prior parameters under the same topic, which means that their probability of appearing in a certain topic is similar. Lexical tags are obtained by binarization of word vectors. At the same time, they can be used as word feature tags according to the way they are generated and combined with conceptual features.

(2) introducing conceptual information. The conceptual information is introduced into the conceptual knowledge network ConceptNet, and the algorithm is designed to improve the biterm generation process of BTM. The Bi-Concept pairs are constructed and sampled on the Bi-Concept set.

As shown in Fig. 1, it is assumed that the corpus set D consists of D documents, in which the vocabulary of each document $d \in \{1, \ldots, D\}$, corpus consists of one word. The vocabulary of each document is processed with the help of the conceptual network to get the Bi-Concept pair set B, and the constructed Bi-Concept pair is the $\{C_i, C_j\}$, concept $n \in \{C_1, \ldots C_i, C_j, \ldots C_n\}$. The arrow in the figure shows the influence relationship on the subsequent parameters. For example, the Vocabulary-word feature label matrix of the word $C_{v,1}$ is deduced according to the distribution of the word v0, and thus affects the Dirichlet priori hyperparameter β_k. BCTM models the topic on the constructed Bi-Concept set, including K topics. V_0, α and β_k are the prior parameters, and the word feature label is L. the generation process is as follows:

(1) for each topic K:
    a. For word feature tags $l \in |L|$, sampling gamma distribution $C_{v,l} \sim Ga(v_0, v_0)$
    b. For the word v, calculate the $\beta_{k,v} = \prod_{l=1}^{L_{word}} c_{l,k}^{C_{v,l}}$
    c. Sampled Dirichlet distribution $\varphi_k \sim Dir(\beta_k)$
(2) for concept pair sets:
    a. Sampled Dirichlet distribution $\theta \sim Dir(\alpha)$
    b. For topic Z, sample category distribution $Z \sim Cat(\theta)$
    c. For conceptual C_n, sampling category distribution $C_n \sim Cat(\varphi_z)$

The symbols and explanations related to the structure of the model are shown in Table 1. It is worth mentioning that in order to integrate the word feature information into the model, the BCTM model uses binary label information to learn a specific Dirichlet prior β_k. That is to say, for any topic extracted from the BCTM model, if the characteristics of the C_i, C_j are similar, then the numerical representation of the corresponding Dirichlet prior β_k on the topic should also be close. This can be understood as: the probability of selecting words with similar features on the same topic is about the same, which is the function of introducing word feature tags. In the end, the sampling of the BCTM model is carried out in the whole set of concept pairs. By constituting the short text into a concept pair set, not only the sparse word co-occurrence information of the original short text can be enriched, but also the accuracy of model modeling can be improved after the introduction of conceptual network.

Table 1. Symbol and meaning of BCTM model

Symbol	Meaning
B	Concept pair set
V	Glossary
K	Number of topics
L	Label dimension
Z	Concept to collection topic
α	Dirichlet prior parameter
θ	The topic distribution of concepts to collections
C_i, C_j	Concept pair
φ_k	Word distribution of topic k
β_k	Dirichlet prior parameter
$C_{l,k}$	Topic-word feature label relevance weight
$C_{v,l}$	Vocabulary-word feature label matrix
v_0	Super parameter

3.2 Introduction of Word Feature Information

At present, the word vectors used in most models can effectively measure the similarity or potential distance between words, but the word vectors can not give the representation of the relationship between words. In order to solve this problem, this paper proposes a binarization word feature label method, which can use word features as external information tags, so that the model sampling process can affect the specific Dirichlet prior corresponding to a topic through labels. In this way, the distribution of words under a topic has a certain law, that is, words with a priori approximation are more likely to appear in the same topic distribution. And then improve the theme consistency of the topic model.

Algorithm 1 word feature label generation algorithm

Input: The word vector set corresponding to the pre-trained vocabulary$G = \{V_1, V_2, \cdots, V_{Count}\}$, where the word vector $V_{count} = \{r_1, r_2, \cdots, r_n\}$

Output:Binary word feature tag set $C' = \{C'_1, C'_2, ..., C'_{Count}\}$, wherein, word feature tag $C'_i = \{c_1, c_2, ..., c_n\}$

For $i = 1, 2, ..., $ Count Do
   For $j = 1, 2, ..., n$ Do
     IF $r_j > 0$ Do
   Word vector positive summation$S_+ += r_j$
     ELSE IF $r_j < 0$ Do
   Summation of negative values of word vectors$S_- += r_j$
     End IF
   End For
   Calculate the positive average $M_+ = S_+/n$ of the word vector V_i
   Calculate the negative average $M_- = S_-/n$ of the word vector V_i
   For $j = 1, 2, ..., n$ Do
     IF $r_j > M_+$ Do
   Current dimension word feature label value$c_j = 1$
       ELSE IF $r_n < M_-$ Do
   Current dimension word feature label value$c_j = 1$
     ELSE Do
   Current dimension word feature label value$c_j = 0$
     End IF
   End For
End For

First, the average M_+, M_-, of the word vector is calculated, where M_+ is the average value of the sum of all positive elements in the word vector, and M_- is the average value of the sum of all negative elements in the word vector. Then, according to whether the value of each dimension of the word vector is positive or negative, it is compared with the calculated average M_+, M_-. According to the comparison of the value of each dimension of the word vector with the calculated average, the operation is performed in turn:

(1) if the current dimension value $> M_+$, the current dimension value $= 1$.
(2) if the current dimension value is less than M_-, the current dimension value is 1.
(3) if it is otherwise, the current dimension value is 0.

The main idea of this method is to retain the "prominent" part of the word vector feature as much as possible, while the more prominent feature refers to the corresponding dimension of the word vector whose value is greater than the average. In this way, the more important features can be retained as much as possible, and the weaker features can be removed at the same time, which can screen the word features to a certain extent and retain the word feature information with good quality. Suppose that the size of the text vocabulary is Count, and the n-dimensional word vector is expressed in the form of $V_i = \{r_1, r_2, \ldots, r_n\}$. In order to make the word feature information can be applied to the model, the binary word feature tag generation algorithm proposed in this paper is shown in Algorithm 1.

At present, many short text topic models combined with word vectors are modeled on the word vector space. Different from those short text topic models, the BCTM model uses word vector tools and introduces word feature information in the form of tags on the basis of the classical topic model to make up for the sparse word co-occurrence of short texts.

3.3 Introduction of Conceptual Information Based on ConceptNet

BCTM model improves the accuracy of topic modeling by introducing concepts as external information. The purpose of constructing Bi-Concept set based on ConceptNet for topic modeling is to improve the quality of the aggregated corpus through high-quality a priori knowledge. However, for the construction of the Bi-Concept collection, we should also pay attention to how to build the concept pair, and the extent to which the concept pair of construction should be extended should also be taken into account. The following will give the algorithm description of the construction of the Bi-Concept used in this paper.

4 Derivation of Parameters

Because the BCTM model introduces the word feature information to sample a corresponding Dirichlet prior for each word. Different from the BTM model, which can not generate document-topic distribution due to the sampling of word pairs, BCTM model modeling is based on the collection of concept pairs, which is equivalent to sampling on the mixed text composed of concept pairs, so it is similar to the sampling process of LDA model.

Given the topic distribution $\theta_{1:D}$ corresponding to a document and the joint distribution of the corresponding word distribution $\varphi_{1:K}$, BCTM model under the topic, the joint distribution can be shown by formulas 1 and 2.

$$P\left(\mathbf{w}_{1:D}, \mathbf{z}_{1:D} | \theta_{1:D}, \varphi_{1:K}\right) = \prod_{d=1}^{D} \prod_{k=1}^{K} \theta_{d, z_{d,i}} \varphi_{z_{d,i}, v} \tag{1}$$

$$\prod_{d=1}^{D} \prod_{k=1}^{K} \theta_{d, z_{d,i}} \varphi_{z_{d,i}, v} = \prod_{d=1}^{D} \prod_{k=1}^{K} \theta_{d,k}^{m_{d,k}} \prod_{d=1}^{D} \prod_{k=1}^{K} \varphi_{k,v}^{n_{k,v}} \tag{2}$$

As shown in the above formula, the modeling method for the corpus set D d $\in$ $\{1, .., D\}$ model is to generate the topics of the document BCTM from the number of topics K, where each topic k $\in \{1, \ldots, K\}$ chooses to generate words from the vocabulary V according to the specific distribution. The BCTM model first samples the topic $z_{d,i} \in \{1, \ldots, K\}$ according to the document-topic distribution $\theta_d \in \mathbb{R}_+^K$, and then samples the lexical $w_{d,i}$ according to the topic-word distribution $\varphi_{z_{d,i}}$. Here $n_{k,v}$ represents the number of v words assigned to topic k, while $m_{d,k}$ refers to the total number of words assigned to topic k by document d. The LDA model uses Dirichlet conjugation to solve the probability distribution, and the solution method here is similar, as shown in formula 3.

$$P(w_{1:D}, z_{1:D} | \alpha_{1:D}, \beta_{1:K}) = \prod_{d=1}^{D} \frac{Beta_K(\alpha_d + m_d)}{Beta_K(\alpha_d)} \prod_{k=1}^{K} \frac{Beta_V(\beta_k + n_k)}{Beta_V(\beta_k)} \tag{3}$$

Algorithm 2 Bi-Concept pair construction algorithm

Input: The $D = \{d_1, d_2, \ldots, d_D\}$, threshold N of the document set to be constructed, and the word collection $V = \{v_1, v_2, \ldots, v_n\}$ of the concept network node set Node $= \{node_1, node_2, \ldots, node_{num}\}$, document d_D

Output: Bi-Concept collection $B = \{b_1, b_2, \ldots, b_D\}$ built by document set D

  For $i = 1, 2, \ldots, D$ **Do**

    For $j = 1, 2, \ldots, n - 1$ **Do**

    Find the starting node $node1$ of v_j corresponding to the conceptual network

    Traversing the conceptual network, constructing the node set $Node' = \{node'_1, node'_2, \ldots, node'_{num}\}$ of $node1$ which can be reachable according to the edge step in the conceptual network.

      For $k = j + 1, j + 2, \ldots, n$ **Do**

      Find the starting node $node2$ of v_k corresponding to the conceptual network

      IF Both $node1$ and $node2$ are in node set b_i **Do**

        Form a Bi-Concept pair of $node1$ and $node2$, and put them into set b_i.

        Put v_j and v_k into set V_C

      End IF

    End For

  End For

  IF The Bi-Concept pair in set b_i is less than the threshold N **Do**

    Remove the vocabulary that appears in V_C in V, and get the vocabulary set $V' = \{v'_1, v'_2, \ldots, v'_m\}$ that does not participate in the formation of Bi-Concept pairs

    For $l = 1, 2, \ldots, m - 1$ **Do**

    Find the starting node $node1'$ of the conceptual network corresponding to v_l

    Traverse the conceptual network and construct the node set $Node'' = \{node''_1, node''_2, \ldots, node''_{count}\}$ that $node1'$ can reach within two steps according to the edge in the conceptual network

      For $g = l + 1, l + 2, \ldots, m$ **Do**

      Find the starting node $node2'$ of the conceptual network corresponding to v_g

      IF Both $node1'$ and $node2'$ are in node set $Node''$ **Do**

        Combine $node1'$ and $node2'$ into a Bi-Concept pair and put them into set b_i

      End IF

      End For

    End For

  End IF

  End For

As shown in formula 3, $\Gamma(\cdot)$ is the gamma function, and $Beta_N(\cdot)$ is the N-dimensional beta function shown in formula 4.

$$Beta_N(x) = \frac{\prod_n \Gamma(x_n)}{\Gamma\left(\sum_n x_n\right)} \tag{4}$$

Assuming that the Dirichlet prior and β for different documents and topics are known, the probability calculation for the assigned topic $z_{d,i}$ d is shown in Formula 5.

$$P(z_{d,i} = k | z_{1:d}^{-Z_{d,i}}, w_{1:D}, \alpha_{1:D}, \beta_{1:K}) \propto (\alpha_{d,k} + m_{d,k}) \frac{\beta_{k,v} + n_{k,v}}{\beta_{k,\cdot} + n_{k,\cdot}} \tag{5}$$

5 Experimental Results and Analysis

As the BCTM model is conceived and implemented with short texts as the main corpus, the corpus adopted in the experiment are all short texts on social media, such as online text fragments, blog content and so on. So far, there is no open and authoritative explanation for the clear definition of short texts, so the experimental corpus is chosen as shorter texts with an average of 15 words, short texts with an average of 100 words, and general texts with an average of more than 1000 words. The reason why we use the dataset with long average vocabulary is that the modeling quality of BCTM model can be verified only from the point of view of short text, although it can reflect the effect of the model to some extent, but because BCTM introduces word feature information and concept information, BCTM model can also achieve good modeling quality in general text modeling. Only from the perspective of short text, there may be some limitations in the quality evaluation of the model, so in the experimental part of the text, several public data sets of three lexical intervals are selected for topic modeling experiments. The specific dataset is described below.

WS (Web-Snippet) [15] dataset. The dataset is widely used in short text topic modeling testing. Contains 12237 Web search fragments. The vocabulary of the dataset contains 10052 words, with an average of 15 words in each segment.

KOS [16] dataset. The data set is obtained from the UCI machine learning database and mainly contains some blog entries and so on. Archambeau et al. used this data set in the experimental part of the model in which the implicit IBP Dirichlet distribution was introduced. It has 3430 documents with a vocabulary of 610 and a vocabulary of 677, with an average of about 100 words per text.

NIPS dataset. The data is also downloaded from UCI machine learning database, and its content is related to NIPS papers. The dataset has 1500 texts, and the glossary contains 12419 words, with an average of about 1266 words in each text.

StackOverFlow [17] dataset. The data set contains 20000 question-and-answer sentences on the StackOverFlow technical question-and-answer website, which are divided into 20 categories for text classification experiments, with an average of about 100 words per text.

Sogou news data set. The data set is the news corpus of Sogou Lab. A total of 1000 texts are selected from each of the five categories of finance and economics, health,

Table 2. Test data set

Data set	Document number	Average document length(words)
Web-Snippet	12237	15
KOS	3430	100
NIPS	1500	1266
StackOverFlow	20000	100
Sogou	1000	80

education, military and culture as a set of training. It is mainly used in text classification experiment, with an average of about 80 words per text (Table 2).

Contrast experiment setting of topic modeling.

The BCTM proposed in this paper is compared with the following methods on the above different data sets.

LDA model, LDA as the most classic topic model, so far there have been many scholars on this basis to improve the model. However, it can not be ignored that the experiment of LDA model on short text and general text is very necessary, because the experimental results are often used as a benchmark to compare with other models. Therefore, this paper also uses LDA as one of the baseline models.

BTM topic model. The most prominent aspect of the BTM model is that it puts forward the idea of transforming the short text corpus into biterm. Different from LDA model, BTM model is sampled based on biterm, so its document-topic distribution needs to be extrapolated to biterm. The advantage of BTM is that it expands the sparse content of short text by constructing biterm collection. Theoretically, the performance of short text should be better than that of LDA model. This paper also adopts the idea of word pairs, so BTM model is also one of the baseline models for comparison.

LF-LDA topic model. The LF-LDA model also introduces the word vector as a supplement to the model to improve the LDA topic model. In the process of topic modeling, LF-LDA introduces the word vector information trained in the large corpus to make the topic randomly select the characteristics of the original text or word vector with a specific distribution, so as to improve the topic consistency of the topic model. This paper also introduces a lot of external information to influence the Dirichlet priori of the text, so the LF-LDA model is also one of the baseline models for comparison.

In this experiment, two mainstream indicators are used to evaluate the quality of a topic model, that is, confusion evaluation [18], topic consistency [19]. Next, we will introduce these evaluation criteria in detail:

The degree of confusion is used to measure the quality of the sample predicted by the probability model. It is an important evaluation index in the field of topic model. The smaller the value of confusion is, the higher the accuracy of the model is.

The confusion evaluation experiments are carried out on three data sets WS, KOS and NIPS, and the BCTM model is compared with the above three models. The results of the comparison are shown in Table 3 below.

Table 3. Comparison of Perplexity of each Model

Data set/$K = 50$	LDA	BTM	LF-LDA	BCTM
WS	923.57	417.98	763.29	**391.61**
KOS	564.58	217.92	286.29	**206.94**
NIPS	431.41	273.23	1098.24	280.34
Data set/$K = 100$	LDA	BTM	LF-LDA	BCTM

(*continued*)

Table 3. (*continued*)

Data set/$K = 50$	LDA	BTM	LF-LDA	BCTM
WS	629.54	302.99	655.81	312.89
KOS	512.38	180.86	269.61	**162.38**
NIPS	431.46	265.71	1083.42	267.53
Data set/$K = 150$	LDA	BTM	LF-LDA	BCTM
WS	501.98	292.41	570.76	**255.24**
KOS	502.54	165.61	231.56	**147.09**
NIPS	431.72	265.70	1074.02	**262.17**
Data set/$K = 200$	LDA	BTM	LF-LFA	BCTM
WS	436.03	236.15	512.81	**198.18**
KOS	496.38	167.29	229.54	**144.01**
NIPS	440.23	265.70	1007.51	**259.70**

From the above table, we can see that on the three data sets of WS, KOS and NIPS, the number of different topics and the degree of confusion calculated by different models are also different. In the table, the models with the least confusion under the same dataset and the same number of topics have been boldly marked. On the whole, the confusion label of BCTM model is relatively low, and the confusion performance of modeling with 50 topics on NIPS data sets, 100 topics on WS data sets and 100 topics on NIPS data sets is not the best. Correspondingly, the best text in these cases is the BTM model. The visualization of the confusion degree experiment on the three corpus is shown in Fig. 2.

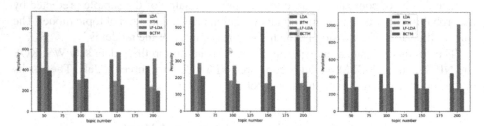

Fig. 2. Schematic diagram of confusion degree of WS, KOS and NIPS datasets

It can be concluded from the graph that due to the introduction of external information, the BCTM model not only expands the content of the text itself, but also improves the performance of confusion compared with the BTM model, and the introduction of word feature information is better for the LF-LDA model. If only in terms of the degree of confusion, the LDA model is the lowest, followed by LF-LDA, and then the best model of BTM, that is, the BCTM model proposed in this paper.

Next, we will evaluate the differences between the BCTM model and the other three models in terms of thematic consistency. Topic consistency calculates the semantic consistency of words that belong to the same topic in the topic model. In the topic model, if the topic consistency is high, it shows that the words within the topic have similar semantics, and the classification effect of the topic model is good. If the consistency of the topic is low, it means that the internal expression of the topic is scattered, and the effect of topic classification is not good. This article uses Normalised Pointwise Mutual Information (NPMI) to measure the consistency of each topic in the topic model, and its formula is shown in formula 6.

$$\sum_{j=2}^{T} \sum_{i=1}^{j-1} log \frac{p(w_j, w_i)}{p(w_j)p(w_i)} / - logp(w_j, w_i) \tag{6}$$

Through this formula, the topic consistency score of topic k based on T high-frequency words in the topic can be calculated. P (w) is the probability of occurrence of word w, $p(w_i, w_j)$ is the probability of simultaneous occurrence of word w_i, w_j in a sliding window. In this experiment, the topic consistency score of each topic k is calculated by the participation of 10 high-frequency words of the topic.

In order to make the theme modeling effect more intuitive, the first ten words of the topic extracted from the BCTM model are mainly displayed. The model has a total of 50 topics, and the first five are shown here. The dataset modeled is KOS. The Table 4 shows.

The content of KOS dataset mainly comes from some topics and contents of blog, so its extracted topics are mostly related to people, events and so on. Take Topic1 as an example, the third word that appears frequently is Wayne, is the name of a character, while the Chinese meanings of the other words are "hand", "drug management", "management" and "debunk". It can be seen from the subject words that the theme should be related to the illegal transactions carried out by a certain character. Topic2 is a theme-word distribution around the subject words such as "government", "law enforcement" and "deadline". Therefore, it can be inferred that the theme should be related to the implementation of laws and regulations of a certain country.

Table 4. TOP10 Vocabulary Presentation of KOS Dataset

Topic1	Topic2	Topic3	Topic4	Topic5
Millers	Grasp	Notably	Handful	Grasp
Hand	Enforcement	Kurds	Journal	Gains
Wayne	Browser	Spoke	Citation	Fundrasin
Drugs	Boulder	Posters	Address	Browser
Manage	Gains	Selection	Violent	Disgruntled
Debunking	Deadline	Implied	Enlisted	Manage
Fixed	Arrogant	Ball	Remained	Recount
Inform	Martin	Boost	Invited	Amendments
Offering	Latif	Judge	Succeed	Childhood
Page	Governmental	Powell	Gains	rallies

The calculation of topic consistency is inseparable from the topic-word matrix generated after the topic modeling, that is, the complete version of the previous Top- vocabulary. The word vector used to judge the contribution probability of topic words is obtained by pre-training the data set extracted from Wiki encyclopedia, and the size is about 5.48G. The specific experimental data are shown in Table 5.

Table 5. Comparison of Theme Consistency Among Models

Data set/$K = 50$	LDA	BTM	LF-LDA	BCTM
WS	−0.028	−0.144	−0.146	**0.023**
KOS	−0.083	−0.098	−0.078	**−0.053**
NIPS	−0.070	−0.087	**0.028**	−0.053
Data set/$K = 100$	LDA	BTM	LF-LDA	BCTM
WS	−0.036	−0.153	−0.152	**−0.001**
KOS	−0.089	−0.090	−0.084	**−0.053**
NIPS	−0.086	−0.002	**−0.010**	−0.046
Data set/$K = 150$	LDA	BTM	LF-LDA	BCTM
WS	−0.033	−0.149	−0.151	**−0.010**
KOS	−0.089	−0.088	−0.075	**−0.051**
NIPS	−0.085	−0.002	**−0.011**	−0.045
Data set/$K = 200$	LDA	BTM	LF-LFA	BCTM
WS	−0.138	−0.148	−0.114	**−0.004**
KOS	−0.089	−0.080	−0.076	**−0.046**
NIPS	−0.037	−0.006	**−0.002**	−0.035

The larger the value of the theme consistency is, the more relevant the subject words of the model are to the topic, and the most prominent experimental results in the table have been bolstered in boldface. As can be seen from Table 5, the BCTM model and the LF-LDA model are more effective in terms of thematic consistency. The topic consistency of the BCTM model is higher on WS datasets and KOS datasets with an average text vocabulary of 10 or 100. BCTM model not only uses word feature information to increase the relevance of subject words, but also introduces conceptual information to model the relationship between words, while BTM and LDA models either enrich text information, but do not enhance the correlation between words, and even introduce additional noise, so the topic consistency scores of these two models are relatively low. In some cases, the LDA model even performs better than the BTM model, which shows that the strong hypothesis of the BTM model does not necessarily play a positive role in the extraction of subject words.

On the whole, from the calculation of Top10 topic words to topic consistency, the comprehensive performance of BCTM model is better in short texts, and it is not weaker than other models in medium-and long-term texts, which verifies the effectiveness of the introduction of external information on topic word extraction.

6 Conclusion

Topic model can effectively extract text features, and has been widely used and studied by industry and academia. With the rapid development of social networks, most of the texts in the network are gradually replaced by short texts, but due to the sparsity of the co-occurrence of short texts, the effect of traditional topic model modeling on short texts is not good. At present, most of the improvements to the short text topic model are carried out through document aggregation and the introduction of word vector features, but ignore high-quality prior knowledge such as conceptual information semantic network. This paper mainly studies the above problems, and completes the following work:

1) A short text topic model BCTM is constructed. BCTM model not only enriches the text content, but also introduces two kinds of external information, word feature information and concept information, into the topic model. At the document level, Bi-Concept sets are constructed for short text by introducing conceptual information, which expands the content of the text and improves the accuracy of modeling by the way of concept pair at the same time. At the modeling level, a special Dirichlet distribution is constructed by introducing word feature information as a priori knowledge, which makes the occurrence probability of similar words under the same topic more similar, thus improving the topic consistency.
2) In this paper, a method of transforming word vectors into binary tags is proposed, and the word feature information is introduced into the BCTM model. In this method, the prominent features of word vectors can be retained, while the weaker features can be discarded. At the same time, in order to apply the generated tags to the model, the topic-word feature tag correlation weight is calculated by introducing a new distribution, and then the influence on the Dirichlet prior parameters in the topic-word matrix is obtained. For each word under the theme, its unique Dirichlet prior parameters are calculated to achieve the purpose of improving topic consistency.
3) In this paper, a method of enriching short text information based on ConceptNet is proposed, and the conceptual information is introduced into the BCTM model. According to the algorithm proposed in this paper, the ConceptNet pair set is constructed according to the algorithm proposed in this paper, and the concept is introduced as external information to improve the accuracy of topic modeling. The BCTM model samples the set on the constructed concept. The follow-up is the parameter derivation of the above-mentioned method.

Although the research work of this paper has improved the quality of modeling in the topic model, the use of external information still needs to be explored. The concept nodes in ConceptNet usually have multiple parts of speech, but this paper takes the noun part of speech to construct Bi-Concept pairs. In the use of ConceptNet network, how to further refine the method of introducing conceptual information into topic modeling by means of part of speech tagging is the future research direction of this paper.

Acknowledgments. This work is supported by Key Research and Development Projects of Heilongjiang Province under grant number GA21C020, and Natural Science Foundation of Heilongjiang Province under grant number LH2021F015.

References

1. Ye, J., Zou, B., Hong, Y., Shen, L., Zhu, Q., Zhou, G.: Negation and speculation scope detection in Chinese. J. Comput. Res. Dev. **56**(7), 1506–1516 (2019). (in Chinese)
2. Blei, D.M., Ng, A.Y., Jordan, M.I.: Latent Dirichlet allocation. J. Mach. Learn. Res. **34**(5), 993–1022 (2003)
3. Liu, Y., Wang, Z., Hou, Y., Yan, H.: A method of extracting malware features based on probabilistic topic model. J. Comput. Res. Dev. **56**(11), 2339–3234 (2019). (in Chinese)
4. Lee, Y.Y., Ke, H., Yen, T.Y., et al.: Combining and learning word embedding with WordNet for semantic relatedness and similarity measurement. J. Am. Soc. Inf. Sci. **71**(6), 657–670 (2020)
5. Limwattana, S., Prom-On, S.: Topic modeling enhancement using word embeddings. In: 2021 18th International Joint Conference on Computer Science and Software Engineering (JCSSE) (2021)
6. Zhao, H., Du, L., Liu, G., et al.: Leveraging meta information in short text aggregation. In: Proceedings of the 57th Annual Meeting of the Association for Computational Linguistics (2019)
7. Yan, X., Guo, J., Lan, Y., et al.: A biterm topic model for short texts. In: Proceedings of the 22nd International Conference on World Wide Web, pp. 1445–1456 (2013)
8. Wu, T., Qi, G., Wang, H., et al.: Cross-Lingual taxonomy alignment with bilingual biterm topic model. In: AAAI, pp. 287–293 (2016)
9. Zhu, Q., Feng, Z., Li, X.: GraphBTM: graph enhanced autoencoded variational inference for biterm topic model. In: Proceedings of the 2018 Conference on Empirical Methods in Natural Language Processing, pp. 4663–4672 (2018)
10. Li, X., Zhang, A., Li, C., et al.: Relational biterm topic model: Short-text topic modeling using word embeddings. Comput. J. **62**(3), 359–372 (2019)
11. Huang, J., Peng, M., Li, P., et al.: Improving biterm topic model with word embeddings. World Wide Web **23**(6), 3099–3124 (2020)
12. Nguyen, D.Q., Billingsley, R., Du, L., et al.: Improving topic models with latent feature word representations. Trans. Assoc. Comput. Linguist. **3**, 299–313 (2015)
13. Li, C., Wang, H., Zhang, Z., et al.: Topic modeling for short texts with auxiliary word embeddings. In: International ACM SIGIR Conference, pp. 165–174. ACM (2016)
14. Gao, W., Peng, M., Wang, H., Zhang, Y., Xie, Q., Tian, G.: Incorporating word embeddings into topic modeling of short text. Knowl. Inf. Syst. **61**(2), 1123–1145 (2018). https://doi.org/10.1007/s10115-018-1314-7
15. Yi, F., Jiang, B., Wu, J.: Topic modeling for short texts via word embedding and document correlation. IEEE Access **PP**(99), 1 (2020)
16. Archambeau, C., Lakshminarayanan, B., Bouchard, G.: Latent IBP compound Dirichlet allocation. IEEE Trans. Pattern Anal. Mach. Intell. **37**(2), 321–333 (2014)
17. Wu, X., Li, C., Zhu, Y., et al.: Short text topic modeling with topic distribution quantization and negative sampling decoder. In: Proceedings of the 2020 Conference on Empirical Methods in Natural Language Processing (EMNLP) (2020)
18. Wallach, H.M., Minmo, D., Mccallum, A.: Rethinking LDA: why priors matter. Adv. Neural. Inf. Process. Syst. **23**, 1973–1981 (2009)
19. Lau, J.H., Newman, D., Baldwin, T.: Machine reading tea leaves: automatically evaluating topic coherence and topic model quality. In: The 14th Conference of the European Chapter of the Association for Computational Linguistics, pp. 530–533 (2014)

An Empirical Study on Model Pruning and Quantization

Yuzhe Tian[1] , Tom H. Luan[2] , and Xi Zheng[1]($\boxtimes$)

[1] School of Computing, Macquarie University, Macquarie Park, NSW 2109, Australia
yuzhe.tian@hdr.mq.edu.au, james.zheng@mq.edu.au
[2] School of Cyber Engineering, Xidian University, Xi'an 710126, Shaanxi, China
tom.luan@xidian.edu.cn

Abstract. In machine learning, model compression is vital for resource-constrained Internet of Things (IoT) devices, such as unmanned aerial vehicles (UAVs) and smart phones. Currently there are some state-of-the-art (SOTA) compression methods, but little study is conducted to evaluate these techniques across different models and datasets. In this paper, we present an in-depth study on two SOTA model compression methods, pruning and quantization. We apply these methods on AlexNet, ResNet18, VGG16BN and VGG19BN, with three well known datasets, *Fashion-MNIST*, *CIFAR-10*, and *UCI-HAR*. Through our study, we draw the conclusion that, applying pruning and retraining could keep the performance (average less than 0.5% degrade) while reducing the model size (at $10\times$ compression rate) on spatial domain datasets (*e.g.* pictures); the performance on temporal domain datasets (*e.g.* motion sensors data) degrades more (average about 5.0% degrade); the performance of quantization is related with the pruning rate and the network architecture. We also compare different clustering methods and reveal the impact on model accuracy and quantization ratio. Finally, we provide some interesting directions for future research.

Keywords: Model compression · Deep neural network · Edge computing

1 Introduction

As the role of Internet of Things (IoT) and edge computing becomes more important, the amount of deployed IoT devices and edge devices keeps growing [39]. These devices are designed for a long period usage even under unattended environments. Thus long battery life becomes the first priority of design, as opposed to the computing abilities. On the other hand, these devices will produce real-time data. It is unrealistic to process these tremendous amount of data acquired by these devices over cloud as the data transmission would require stable internet connection and efficient bandwidth, and consume considerable amount of power.

© ICST Institute for Computer Sciences, Social Informatics and Telecommunications Engineering 2023
Published by Springer Nature Switzerland AG 2023. All Rights Reserved
W. Wang and J. Wu (Eds.): BROADNETS 2023, LNICST 511, pp. 111–125, 2023.
https://doi.org/10.1007/978-3-031-40467-2_7

This is against the real-time processing, power efficiency and network tolerance requirements of IoT devices. For instance, fatigue detection during driving needs to respond in real-time for live saving [27]. Unmanned aerial vehicles (UAVs) require power efficiency to conduct long term tasks without power recharge [14]. Human activities detection would require long term wearing without interrupt users' daily life [4,10,25,26]. Offshore oil platforms usually contain considerable IoT devices but the devices' connection to Internet is limited [30]. Industrial control systems require real-time response for monitoring and security [13,34].

Conversely, as the main focus of current research is targeted on increasing model accuracy, modern deep neural networks usually contain dozens to hundreds of layers, e.g. MobileNet [19] and Vision Transformer (ViT) [12]. The corresponding model parameters have also proportionally increased, which leads to a large model size. Though these models could perform well, they require a substantial computing resources to deploy. For instance, the size of commonly used pre-trained model VGG19 [32] is 550MB, while the onboard random access memory (RAM) of Raspberry Pico is only 264KB[1]. Not only the IoT devices, modern edge devices, e.g. micro controller units (MCUs) and mobile phones, are also limited by their battery capacity and computing resources. Table 1 shows a comparison of commonly used model sizes against mainstream edge devices memory capacity.

Table 1. Model size/hardware memory comparison.

Network	Model Size[d]	B1[a]	B2[a]	B3[a]	SW1[b]	SW2[b]	M1[c]	M2[c]
		Memory Capacity						
ResNet18	$\approx 45MB$	32 KB	32 KB	8 MB	1 GB	1.5 GB	6 GB	8GB
AlexNet	≈235 MB							
VGG11	≈500 MB							
VGG19	≈550 MB							

[a] B1: Arduino MKR1010, B2: Arduino Portenta H7,
B3: Raspberry Pi Zero
[b] SW1: Apple Watch Series 8, SW2: Samsung Galaxy Watch 4
[c] M1: iPhone 13 Pro Max, M2: Samsung Galaxy 22 Ultra
[d] https://pytorch.org/docs/stable/hub.html

Thus, these accurate but sizeable models need to be compressed before deployed. Recent research proposed several approaches to perform model compression, e.g. parameter pruning and quantization [16], low-rank factorization [11,28] and knowledge distillation (KD) [3]. In 2015, Han et al. [16] proposed Deep Compression, which applied pruning, quantization, and Huffman coding on LeNet, AlexNet and VGG-16 networks, with the max compression rate 35× (2.88% of the original size) for AlexNet and 49× (2.04% of the original size) for VGG-16 without impacting the model accuracy. In 2014, Denton et al. [11]

---

[1] https://www.raspberrypi.com/documentation/microcontrollers/raspberry-pi-pico. html.

noted that, within a Convolution Neural Network (CNN), nearly 90% of the computing time are spent on conv layers, while the first several layers are the most time-consuming ones. By using low rank approximation, which decomposes the original parameter matrices with Singular Value Decomposition (SVD), the required space for matrices storage could be significantly decreased. Moreover, the decomposed matrices could be clustered, and the method reaches a final compression rate at 3.9×. In 2014, Ba and Caruana [3] proposed knowledge distillation, which trained a shallow network to mimic a deep network, without sacrificing accuracy. This method was based on one of the authors' previous work [5], which trained a small network to approximate a full network on pseudo data.

However, these methods are limited on particular networks or datasets, *e.g.* LeNet, AlexNet, *MNIST*, or even on pseudo data. Meanwhile, with the advancement of neural network theory and design, modern networks contain complex architectures and layers to extract features from large datasets. Apply the compression methods directly to complex modern networks may lead to poor performance. It is necessary to investigate the capabilities, as current researches lack the exploration of the applicability of these compression methods on modern models and datasets. Thus, we present this work, in which we apply two state-of-the-art (SOTA) compression methods on different models and datasets, provide an in-depth comparison of the method performance on different models along with different datasets. We also show the understanding of both limitations and possibilities of the model compression techniques, which indicates the research directions in the future.

To summarize, this study makes the following major contributions:

- By comprehensive experiments of two SOTA model compression techniques, we propose a general guideline for applying compression methods on modern models;
- Within the empirical study, we apply one SOTA compression method (quantization) progressively, probe the limitation, compare different clustering methods, and reveal the impact in great detail.
- We open-source our implementation on GitHub[2], which could benefit the community for future researches.

The remainder of this paper is structured as follows. In Sect. 2, we introduce the techniques we apply for the experiments. In Sect. 3, we present the empirical study results and our discussion. In Sect. 4, we review the related work. In Sect. 5, we draw the conclusion and point out our future research direction.

---

[2] https://github.com/paul-tian/broadnets2022-compression.

2 Methodology

2.1 Data Augmentation

To increase the generalization of deep learning models, there are two major approaches, one on models architecture, and the other on training datasets [31]. Commonly used model-side techniques add specific functions to the models, *e.g.* dropout [33] and batch normalization [21], while commonly used data augmentation (images) methods are geometric transformations, flipping, color space alteration, cropping, rotation, and noise injection [31].

As our research target is to explore the compression effectiveness on specific models, we choose to augment the training datasets to help mitigate overfitting. In our experiments, the image datasets, *Fashion-MNIST* and *CIFAR-10*, are both augmented with the procedure shown in Fig. 1.

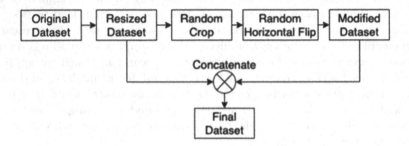

Fig. 1. Dataset augmentation procedure.

The augmentation step adopts from the practice in [18]. As our implementation of networks requires constant input shape, we first reshape the image to the required size, 63×63 for AlexNet [24], 33×33 for ResNet 18 [18], 32×32 for VGG-11 [32] with Batch Normalization [21] and VGG-19 [32] with Batch Normalization [21]. A random crop is sampled, follows by a random horizontal flip with 0.5 as the possibility. It is worth noting that the random crop is padding-enabled to maintain the required size.

2.2 Pruning

Model pruning will remove certain weights from the network, which could help reduce the amount of parameters, while keep the performance degradation in an acceptable level. The pruning method we apply to the chosen models is adopted from Han *et al.* [16]. We train the chosen models from scratch, prune these models with different thresholds, and evaluate the consequence of different compression rates.

The pruning threshold is calculated as:

$$\mathcal{T} = STD(W_l) \times Sensitivity \tag{1}$$

where $\mathcal{T}$ stands for the pruning threshold, STD stands for standard deviation, and W_l stands for weights per layer.

Sensitivity is a hyperparameter, by adjusting it, we could tune the pruning ratio and explore through different compression rates.

The pruning procedure is shown as Fig. 2.

Fig. 2. Train, prune, retrain.

2.3   Quantization

After the pruning, the weight matrices could still be compressed through quantization. We choose to perform weight sharing as a method of quantization, which will cluster weight values and use the value of centroids as the representative value for the weights in the same clustering. An example of weight sharing is shown in Fig. 3. Though there are several clustering centroid initialization methods (e.g. random [29], density-based [9], linear [7]), it has been proved that initializing the centroids with linear method could mitigate poor representation caused by the singular value [16]. However, the limitation of the linear centroids lacks discovery. Thus, we investigate the boundary of the linear centroid method in terms of compression ratio and accuracy. We also investigate modern non-linear method and conduct comparison.

The linear centroids of weights clustering can be calculated as:

$$Centroids = Cluster(2^{Q\text{-}Bit}, W_l) \tag{2}$$

where the Q_Bit stands for the quantization bits, which is a hyperparameter, $Cluster$ stands for the clustering algorithm, and W_l stands for weights per layer.

The non-linear centroids of weights clustering can be calculated as:

$$Centroids = Cluster(W_l) \tag{3}$$

where W_l stands for weights per layer. As the centroids initialization in this non-linear method is value-based, no centroid value is required for input.

3   Experiments

3.1   Experimental Setup

Dataset: The experiments are conducted based on three widely used datasets, *Fashion-MNIST*[3] [40], *CIFAR-10*[4] [23], and *UCI-HAR*[5] [1]. ***Fashion-MNIST***

---

[3] https://github.com/zalandoresearch/fashion-mnist.
[4] https://www.cs.toronto.edu/~kriz/cifar.html.
[5] https://archive.ics.uci.edu/ml/datasets/human+activity+recognition+using
+smartphones.

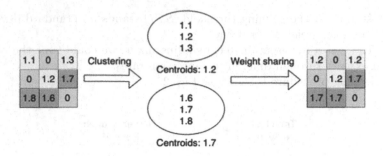

Fig. 3. An example of non-zero weight sharing. There are 6 non-zero weights in this 3×3 weight matrix. $1.1, 1.2, 1.3$ are clustered to 1.2, and $1.6, 1.7, 1.8$ are clustered to 1.7. The new weight matrix is then generated by replacing the original number with the clustered one.

dataset is an image dataset of Zalando's article images, with a training set of 60,000 examples and a test set of 10,000 examples. Each example is a 28×28 grayscale image, associated with a label from 10 different classes. *CIFAR-10* dataset consists of 60,000 colour images, with a training set of 50,000 examples and a test set of 10,000 examples. Each example is a 32×32 grayscale image, associated with a label from 10 classes. *UCI-HAR* dataset is a human activities dataset. It is built from the recordings of 30 study participants, aged from 19 to 48, performing activities of daily living (ADL). The data are collected by a waist-mounted smartphone (Samsung Galaxy S II) with embedded inertial sensors. This dataset contains six ADL, *i.e.* WALKING, WALKINGUPSTAIRS, WALK-INGDOWNSTAIRS, SITTING, STANDING and LAYING. The sampling rate of the inertial sensors (*i.e.* accelerometer and gyroscope) 50 Hz, and the labels are tagged manually with respect to the video recording. The sensor signals are pre-processed with noise-filtering and sampled through fixed-width (128 readings per window) sliding windows.

Evaluated Neural Networks: The aim of this experiment is to investigate the feasibility of the network compression method in different SOTA neural networks. The chosen neural networks are ResNet 18 [18], AlexNet [24], VGG-11 [32] with Batch Normalization [21] (**VGG11BN**), and VGG-19 [32] with Batch Normalization [21] (**VGG19BN**), which have 11.2M, 20.3M, 28.1M, 40.0M parameters, respectively.

Training: All experiments are implemented using Pytorch (version 1.11.0) with CUDA (version 11) on a single NVIDIA RTX 2080Ti GPU. The experimental hyperparameter settings are illustrated in Table 2.

Table 2. Experimental hyperparameter setting.

Hyperparameter description	Values
Number of training epochs	100
Batch size	64
Spatial learning rate[a]	0.01 with a decay rate = 0.1 per 20 epochs
Temporal learning rate[b]	0.001 with a decay rate = 0.1 per 30 epochs
Random seed	42
Optimizer	SGD with default setting
Weight initialization	Kaiming He Initialization [17]

[a] Learning rate for spatial domain datasets, *i.e. Fashion-MNIST* and *CIFAR-10*.
[b] Learning rate for temporal domain datasets, *i.e. UCI-HAR*.

3.2 Research Questions

- **RQ1: How the weight-based pruning affects the models' performance?**
  We first train the full networks from plain, then apply the weight-based pruning on the backbone networks with different pruning rates $\{-10\%, -50\%, -90\%\}$. The corresponding compression rates are $\{1.1\times, 2\times, 10\times\}$, respectively.
- **RQ2: How the various compression rates affect the models' performance if retraining the model?**
  We retrain the various pruned networks with the same training settings as the full ones.
- **RQ3: How the various quantization storage bits affect the models' performance, and what is the modern non-linear centroids initialization performance?**
  We quantize the non-zero weights with different storage bits settings (hyperparameter Q_Bit). The corresponding centroid numbers for different Q_Bit $\{4, 3, 2\}$ are $\{2^4, 2^3, 2^2\}$, respectively. We also apply a modern non-linear clustering centroid initialization (K-Means++ [2]) along with the linear clustering centroid initialization for comparison.

3.3 Experiment Results

In order to explore the impact and suitability of model compression on different networks, we perform extensive experiments on the selected neural networks. The pruning results for the three datasets, *Fashion-MNIST*, *CIFAR-10* and *UCI-HAR*, are shown in Table 3, 4, 5, respectively. The quantization results are shown in Table 6.

For **RQ1**, comparing with the full models, the performance of compressed ones degrade by 2.33% on *Fashion-MNIST* dataset, 4.25% on *CIFAR-10*, 41.57% on *UCI-HAR*, on average, with 2× models. While 73.19% on *Fashion-MNIST* dataset, 62.88% on *CIFAR-10*, 67.29% on *UCI-HAR*, on average, with 10× models. The 1.1× models show no significant difference. This phenomenon shows that pure pruning could still keep the model performance until 2×, but models for temporal domain datasets are more vulnerable to pruning.

Table 3. Pruning result comparison, *Fashion-MNIST*.

Network	Sensitivity[a]	#Params	Comp. Rate[b]	Acc-AP[c]	Acc[d]
ResNet18	–	11.2M	1×	–	93.27
	0.111	10.1M	1.1×	93.26	93.27
	0.609	5.6M	2×	90.81	93.10
	1.590	1.1M	10×	29.04	93.05
AlexNet	–	20.3M	1×	–	92.91
	0.127	18.3M	1.1×	92.89	92.90
	0.671	10.2M	2×	89.01	92.78
	1.510	2.0M	10×	21.61	92.45
VGG11BN	–	28.1M	1×	–	94.39
	0.095	25.3M	1.1×	94.31	94.26
	0.528	14.1M	2×	92.00	94.23
	1.499	2.8M	10×	17.92	94.22
VGG19BN	–	40.0M	1×	–	93.98
	0.102	35.0M	1.1×	93.97	93.98
	0.557	19.5M	2×	93.40	93.85
	1.510	3.9M	10×	13.22	93.61

[a] The pruning sensitivity.
[b] The compression rate.
[c] The accuracy after pruning without retrain. (**RQ1**)
[d] The accuracy after training (**full network**)/retraining (**pruned network**). (**RQ2**)

It is also noticeable that, though pruning will lead to model performance degradation, different pruning rates will lead to opposite performance. On spatial domain datasets (*Fashion-MNIST* and *CIFAR-10*), VGG19BN, the biggest network among the 4 chosen networks, shows the least degrade (less than 1%) for 2× compression, while the largest degrade (more than 78%) occurs for 10× compression. In contrast, ResNet18, the smallest network, shows the largest degradation (more than 4%, the same as AlexNet) for 2× compression, while the least degradation (less than 63%) for 10× compression. We believe that for large networks with considerable feature extraction layers, the stability could maintain when pruning. But when certain portions of the weights are removed, the performance will drastically drop. For residual networks, the feature extraction layers are shallow, but the structure makes them more restrainable when a large number of weights are pruned (*i.e.* 90%). In other words, large deep networks are insensitive but vulnerable to pruning. Meanwhile, residual networks are sensitive but robust for pruning. On the temporal domain dataset (*UCI-HAR*), though AlexNet shows the least degradation among all chosen networks, all four networks show obvious degradation starting from 2× compression. We believe that models trained for temporal domain datasets are more fragile and susceptible to pruning.

For **RQ2**, from Table 3, 4, 5, after retraining the pruned networks, the performance of all compressed networks (*i.e.* 1.1×, 2×, 10×) shows no noticeable

Table 4. Pruning result comparison, *CIFAR-10*.

Network	Sensitivity[a]	#Params	Comp. Rate[b]	Acc-AP[c]	Acc[d]
ResNet18	–	11.2M	1×	–	83.88
	0.111	10.1M	1.1×	83.17	83.81
	0.633	5.6M	2×	77.55	83.51
	1.437	1.1M	10×	42.37	83.21
AlexNet	–	20.3M	1×	–	82.39
	0.137	18.3M	1.1×	82.16	82.39
	0.718	10.2M	2×	76.49	82.38
	1.520	2.0M	10×	18.43	81.98
VGG11BN	–	28.1M	1×	–	88.76
	0.100	25.3M	1.1×	88.46	88.73
	0.552	14.1M	2×	85.29	88.67
	1.510	2.8M	10×	19.94	88.14
VGG19BN	–	40.0M	1×	–	90.33
	0.107	35.0M	1.1×	89.80	90.23
	0.582	19.5M	2×	89.01	90.22
	1.535	3.9M	10×	13.11	89.75

[a] The pruning sensitivity.
[b] The compression rate.
[c] The accuracy after pruning without retrain. (**RQ1**)
[d] The accuracy after training (**full network**)/retraining (**pruned network**). (**RQ2**)

Table 5. Pruning result comparison, *UCI-HAR*.

Network	Sensitivity[a]	#Params	Comp. Rate[b]	Acc-AP[c]	Acc[d]
ResNet18	–	11.2M	1×	–	86.97
	0.126	10.1M	1.1×	85.44	85.51
	0.684	5.6M	2×	51.68	84.43
	1.709	1.1M	10×	16.66	82.80
AlexNet	–	20.3M	1×	–	83.17
	0.175	18.3M	1.1×	80.69	83.10
	0.888	10.2M	2×	68.88	82.15
	1.601	2.0M	10×	23.82	71.71
VGG11BN	–	28.1M	1×	–	85.44
	0.126	25.3M	1.1×	84.70	84.80
	0.678	14.1M	2×	32.85	84.36
	1.668	2.8M	10×	14.25	84.05
VGG19BN	–	40.0M	1×	–	84.29
	0.126	35.0M	1.1×	84.19	84.19
	0.678	19.5M	2×	20.20	83.37
	1.663	3.9M	10×	15.98	81.68

[a] The pruning sensitivity.
[b] The compression rate.
[c] The accuracy after pruning without retrain. (**RQ1**)
[d] The accuracy after training (**full network**)/retraining (**pruned network**). (**RQ2**)

or tolerable degradation (average degrade is less than 0.7% on spatial domain datasets and 4.9% on temporal domain datasets, maximum 0.62% and 11.46%, respectively). This reflects that retraining is essential for high compression rates (*e.g.* 10×), and applying retraining step could keep the overall accuracy.

For **RQ3**, from Table 6, the performance degradation for 4 quantization bits (Q_Bit {4}) is not noticeable (average less than 1%, minimum 0.04% and maximum 1.92%). For Q_Bit {2}, all the evaluated neural networks show fatal performance degradation, which indicates that quantization with {2} (*i.e.* 2^2, or 4 unique numbers as clustering centroids) cannot maintain a usable status for model quantization. It is worth noting that, for deep networks (*i.e.* ResNet18 and VGG19BN), the performance of quantization correlates to the pruning rate. The higher the pruning rate, the higher the quantization performance. We believe the reason is that, small-value weights will become the noise for clustering and degrade the performance worse. The increasing pruning rate can reduce the noise and help mitigate the performance degradation. On the contrary, for shallow networks (*i.e.* AlexNet and VGG11BN), the performance of quantization is related not only to the pruning rate, but also to the Q_Bit value. When Q_Bit is lower than {4}, the quantization performance is in inverse proportion to the pruning rate. When Q_Bit equals {4}, it shows a similar characteristic as deep networks. We believe the reason is that, shallow networks contain fewer layers and the distinctiveness of parameters is the key to maintaining the performance. Applying quantization with fewer clustering centroids will destroy the distinctiveness and degrade the performance. While deep networks contain enough layers, which is more robust for the distinctiveness loss after the quantization. It is also worth noting that, ResNet18 performs the best among all four networks. As ResNet18 contains residual block (RESBLOCK), which might be the key part for maintaining the accuracy.

4   Related Work

Since AlexNet [24] won the 2012 ImageNet competition, Convolutional Networks have become more accurate by growing larger. However, deep Convolutional Neural Networks are often overparameterized, which has led to researchers attempting to reduce model size by trading accuracy for efficiency.

Handcraft Efficient Mobile-Size Convolutional Networks: It is a common solution to handcraft efficient mobile-size Convolution Networks, such as SqueezeNets [20], and ShuffleNets [42]. One of the most famous models is MobileNet [19], which proposes depthwise separable convolutions to build light weight deep neural networks. This work introduces two simple global hyperparameters that efficiently trade off between latency and accuracy. These hyperparameters allow the model builder to choose the right sized model for their application based on the constraints of the problem. Comparing with model compression, this solution is also possible to deploy a high-accurate neural network on IoT devices, which could be an efficient way for solving particular tasks. However, to design a network from scratch requires considerable time and com-

An Empirical Study on Model Pruning and Quantization   121

Table 6. Quantization result comparison.

		AlexNet				ResNet18	
P-Rate[a]	Q_Bit[b]	Deg-L[c](%)	Deg-NL[d](%)	P-Rate[a]	Q_Bit[b]	Deg-L[c](%)	Deg-NL[d](%)
	2	23.74	20.90		2	62.70	68.43
1.1×	3	3.48	5.34	1.1×	3	8.19	9.68
	4	1.04	0.77		4	0.17	0.50
	2	23.07	36.62		2	47.61	58.43
2×	3	3.51	4.45	2×	3	2.29	3.28
	4	0.28	0.65		4	0.67	0.68
	2	32.63	42.07		2	43.79	39.12
10×	3	6.42	7.45	10×	3	1.92	3.02
	4	0.30	0.09		4	0.19	0.66

		VGG11BN				VGG19BN	
P-Rate[a]	Q_Bit[b]	Deg-L[c](%)	Deg-NL[d](%)	P-Rate[a]	Q_Bit[b]	Deg-L[c](%)	Deg-NL[d](%)
	2	62.41	73.75		2	57.22	77.55
1.1×	3	18.69	16.72	1.1×	3	34.84	35.55
	4	0.94	0.55		4	0.12	1.32
	2	48.37	75.19		2	77.33	77.33
2×	3	2.66	2.08	2×	3	12.21	16.32
	4	0.24	0.04		4	0.42	0.29
	2	52.80	67.86		2	71.38	77.09
10×	3	2.94	3.44	10×	3	3.46	5.18
	4	0.31	0.50		4	0.06	0.04

[a] The model of corresponding compression rate from pruning.
[b] The quantization bit for storing the shared weight.
[c] The average accuracy degrade for linear clustering centroid initialization.
[d] The average accuracy degrade for non-linear clustering centroid initialization

puting resources, while model compression could directly leverage existing, high-maturity neural networks with small efforts.

Neural Architecture Search for Efficient Mobile-Size Convolutional Networks: Recently, neural architecture search has become increasingly popular in the design of efficient mobile-sized Convolutional Networks [6,35], and can achieve even better performances than hand-crafted mobile Convolutional Networks by carefully tuning the width, depth, size, and type of convolution kernels. EfficientNet [36] is one of the typical models which scales the networks to small their size. EfficientNet uses fixed scaling coefficients to uniformly scale width, depth, and resolution of networks. It is noteworthy that their scaling method can also be applied to MobileNet and ResNet. Compared with other single-dimension scaling methods [18,19,41], their compound scaling method performs better on all of these models. It is also possible to combine this method with model compression for even smaller computing requirement and higher efficiency (*e.g.* we apply the compression on ResNet in the experimentation).

Others Researches on Model Compression: In 2020, Yu et al. [8] reviewed recent model compression techniques, and classified them as **Pruning, Quantization, Low-rank Approximation**, and **Knowledge Distillation**. Low rank approximation could decompose the original parameter matrices with SVD and decrease the required matrices storage space, while knowledge distillation researches the target by training a shallow network to mimic a deep one, instead of altering the original network itself.

Other Researches on Splitting Models: As edge devices play an vital role in IoT, one possible methodology of deploying the deep neural networks on them are model splitting. Inference models are spitted by layers, and the execution framework will schedule the layers execution and transfer the layer output through internet connection [15,22,38]. By leveraging the strong cloud computing abilities and internet connection (*e.g.* Wi-Fi, LTE and 5G), model splitting could significantly improve the network efficiency, comparing with pure local computing or cloud computing.

5 Conclusion

It this work, we practice the pruning and quantization compression empirical study towards a popular SOTA method. We reveal the advantages of the SOTA method, *e.g.* pruning 10× with no noticeable performance degrade (less than 0.7%) and quantization with 2^3 with acceptable degrade (less than 5.0%) on spatial domain datasets (*i.e. Fashion-MNIST* and *CIFAR-10*); while the performance temporal domain datasets (*i.e. UCI-HAR*) degrades more (maximum 15.55%). Meanwhile, we compare different clustering algorithms and improve the performance (maximum 0.5%, on AlexNet 10×). We have open-sourced these experimentation codes on GitHub[6]. Based on the well performance of graph neural networks on non-euclidean distance datasets, we plan on further explore the compatible compression methods towards graph neural networks. It is worth noting that, in recent years, other methods for deploying neural networks on IoT devices appear, from both compression aspect (*e.g.* knowledge distillation, low-rank approximation and transfer learning) and execution aspect (*e.g.* model splitting). These new approaches provide us a horizon of researching. Meanwhile, as transformer networks (i.e. [12,37]) also contain residual blocks as ResNet18, it is possible to apply model compression on transformer networks with high P-Rate (*e.g.* 10×) and $Q\_Bit\{4\}$ to reach a high compression rate while maintaining the performance. We also plan on further explore the boundaries of these methods.

---

[6] https://github.com/paul-tian/broadnets2022-compression.

Acknowledgements. This work is in part supported by an Australian Research Council (ARC) Discovery Project (DP210102447), an ARC Linkage Project (LP190100676), and a DATA61 project (Data61 CRP C020996).

References

1. Anguita, D., Ghio, A., Oneto, L., Parra Perez, X., Reyes Ortiz, J.L.: A public domain dataset for human activity recognition using smartphones. In: Proceedings of the 21th International European Symposium on Artificial Neural Networks, Computational Intelligence and Machine Learning, pp. 437–442 (2013)
2. Arthur, D., Vassilvitskii, S.: k-means++: the advantages of careful seeding. Technical report, Stanford (2006)
3. Ba, J., Caruana, R.: Do deep nets really need to be deep? Adv. Neural Inf. Process. Syst. **27** (2014)
4. Bhandari, B., Lu, J., Zheng, X., Rajasegarar, S., Karmakar, C.: Non-invasive sensor based automated smoking activity detection. In: 2017 39th Annual International Conference of the IEEE Engineering in Medicine and Biology Society (EMBC), pp. 845–848. IEEE (2017)
5. Buciluă, C., Caruana, R., Niculescu-Mizil, A.: Model compression. In: Proceedings of the 12th ACM SIGKDD International Conference on Knowledge Discovery and Data Mining, pp. 535–541 (2006)
6. Cai, H., Zhu, L., Han, S.: ProxylessNAS: direct neural architecture search on target task and hardware. arXiv preprint arXiv:1812.00332 (2018)
7. Celebi, M.E., Kingravi, H.A.: Linear, deterministic, and order-invariant initialization methods for the K-means clustering algorithm. In: Celebi, M.E. (ed.) Partitional Clustering Algorithms, pp. 79–98. Springer, Cham (2015). https://doi.org/10.1007/978-3-319-09259-1_3
8. Cheng, Y., Wang, D., Zhou, P., Zhang, T.: A survey of model compression and acceleration for deep neural networks. arXiv preprint arXiv:1710.09282 (2017)
9. Dalhatu, K., Sim, A.T.H.: Density base k-mean's cluster centroid initialization algorithm. Int. J. Comput. Appl. **137**(11) (2016)
10. Deep, S., Tian, Y., Lu, J., Zhou, Y., Zheng, X.: Leveraging multi-view learning for human anomaly detection in industrial internet of things. In: 2020 International Conferences on Internet of Things (iThings) and IEEE Green Computing and Communications (GreenCom) and IEEE Cyber, Physical and Social Computing (CPSCom) and IEEE Smart Data (SmartData) and IEEE Congress on Cybermatics (Cybermatics), pp. 533–537. IEEE (2020)
11. Denton, E.L., Zaremba, W., Bruna, J., LeCun, Y., Fergus, R.: Exploiting linear structure within convolutional networks for efficient evaluation. Adv. Neural Inf. Process. Syst. **27** (2014)
12. Dosovitskiy, A., et al.: An image is worth 16×16 words: transformers for image recognition at scale. arXiv preprint arXiv:2010.11929 (2020)
13. Drias, Z., Serhrouchni, A., Vogel, O.: Analysis of cyber security for industrial control systems. In: 2015 International Conference on Cyber Security of Smart Cities, Industrial Control System and Communications (SSIC), pp. 1–8. IEEE (2015)
14. Fujii, K., Higuchi, K., Rekimoto, J.: Endless flyer: a continuous flying drone with automatic battery replacement. In: 2013 IEEE 10th International Conference on Ubiquitous Intelligence and Computing and 2013 IEEE 10th International Conference on Autonomic and Trusted Computing, pp. 216–223. IEEE (2013)

15. Han, S., Shen, H., Philipose, M., Agarwal, S., Wolman, A., Krishnamurthy, A.: MCDNN: an approximation-based execution framework for deep stream processing under resource constraints. In: Proceedings of the 14th Annual International Conference on Mobile Systems, Applications, and Services, pp. 123–136 (2016)

16. Han, S., Mao, H., Dally, W.J.: Deep compression: compressing deep neural networks with pruning, trained quantization and Huffman coding. arXiv preprint arXiv:1510.00149 (2015)

17. He, K., Zhang, X., Ren, S., Sun, J.: Delving deep into rectifiers: surpassing human-level performance on ImageNet classification. In: Proceedings of the IEEE International Conference on Computer Vision, pp. 1026–1034 (2015)

18. He, K., Zhang, X., Ren, S., Sun, J.: Deep residual learning for image recognition. In: Proceedings of the IEEE Conference on Computer Vision and Pattern Recognition, pp. 770–778 (2016)

19. Howard, A.G., et al.: MobileNets: efficient convolutional neural networks for mobile vision applications. arXiv preprint arXiv:1704.04861 (2017)

20. Iandola, F.N., Han, S., Moskewicz, M.W., Ashraf, K., Dally, W.J., Keutzer, K.: SqueezeNet: AlexNet-level accuracy with 50x fewer parameters and <0.5 mb model size. arXiv preprint arXiv:1602.07360 (2016)

21. Ioffe, S., Szegedy, C.: Batch normalization: accelerating deep network training by reducing internal covariate shift. In: International Conference on Machine Learning, pp. 448–456. PMLR (2015)

22. Kang, Y., Hauswald, J., Gao, C., Rovinski, A., Mudge, T., Mars, J., Tang, L.: Neurosurgeon: collaborative intelligence between the cloud and mobile edge. ACM SIGARCH Comput. Archit. News $45(1)$, 615–629 (2017)

23. Krizhevsky, A.: Learning multiple layers of features from tiny images (2009)

24. Krizhevsky, A., Sutskever, I., Hinton, G.E.: ImageNet classification with deep convolutional neural networks. Adv. Neural Inf. Process. Syst. 25 (2012)

25. Lu, J., Wang, J., Zheng, X., Karmakar, C., Rajasegarar, S.: Detection of smoking events from confounding activities of daily living. In: Proceedings of the Australasian Computer Science Week Multiconference, pp. 1–9 (2019)

26. Lu, J., Zheng, X., Sheng, M., Jin, J., Yu, S.: Efficient human activity recognition using a single wearable sensor. IEEE Internet Things J. $7(11)$, 11137–11146 (2020)

27. Lu, J., et al.: Can steering wheel detect your driving fatigue? IEEE Trans. Veh. Technol. $70(6)$, 5537–5550 (2021)

28. Lu, Y., Kumar, A., Zhai, S., Cheng, Y., Javidi, T., Feris, R.: Fully-adaptive feature sharing in multi-task networks with applications in person attribute classification. In: Proceedings of the IEEE Conference on Computer Vision and Pattern Recognition, pp. 5334–5343 (2017)

29. MacQueen, J., et al.: Some methods for classification and analysis of multivariate observations. In: Proceedings of the Fifth Berkeley Symposium on Mathematical Statistics and Probability, Oakland, CA, USA, vol. 1, pp. 281–297 (1967)

30. Mammadova, M., Jabrayilova, Z.: Conceptual approaches to IoT-based personnel health management in offshore oil and gas industry. Control Optim. Industr. Appl. 257 (2020)

31. Shorten, C., Khoshgoftaar, T.M.: A survey on image data augmentation for deep learning. J. Big Data $6(1)$, 1–48 (2019)

32. Simonyan, K., Zisserman, A.: Very deep convolutional networks for large-scale image recognition. arXiv preprint arXiv:1409.1556 (2014)

33. Srivastava, N., Hinton, G., Krizhevsky, A., Sutskever, I., Salakhutdinov, R.: Dropout: a simple way to prevent neural networks from overfitting. J. Mach. Learn. Res. $15(1)$, 1929–1958 (2014)

34. Sung, W.T., Hsu, Y.C.: Designing an industrial real-time measurement and monitoring system based on embedded system and ZigBee. Expert Syst. Appl. **38**(4), 4522–4529 (2011)

35. Tan, M., et al.: MnasNet: platform-aware neural architecture search for mobile. In: Proceedings of the IEEE/CVF Conference on Computer Vision and Pattern Recognition, pp. 2820–2828 (2019)

36. Tan, M., Le, Q.: EfficientNet: rethinking model scaling for convolutional neural networks. In: International Conference on Machine Learning, pp. 6105–6114. PMLR (2019)

37. Vaswani, A., et al.: Attention is all you need. Adv. Neural Inf. Process. Syst. **30** (2017)

38. Wang, S., Zhang, X., Uchiyama, H., Matsuda, H.: Hivemind: towards cellular native machine learning model splitting. IEEE J. Sel. Areas Commun. **40**(2), 626–640 (2021)

39. Wang, T., et al.: Mobile edge-enabled trust evaluation for the internet of things. Inf. Fusion **75**, 90–100 (2021)

40. Xiao, H., Rasul, K., Vollgraf, R.: Fashion-MNIST: a novel image dataset for benchmarking machine learning algorithms (2017)

41. Zagoruyko, S., Komodakis, N.: Wide residual networks. arXiv preprint arXiv:1605.07146 (2016)

42. Zhang, X., Zhou, X., Lin, M., Sun, J.: ShuffleNet: an extremely efficient convolutional neural network for mobile devices. In: Proceedings of the IEEE Conference on Computer Vision and Pattern Recognition, pp. 6848–6856 (2018)

Client Selection Based on Diversity Scaling for Federated Learning on Non-IID Data

Yuechao Ren$^{(\boxtimes)}$ (iD), Atul Sajjanhar (iD), Shang Gao (iD), and Seng Loke (iD)

Deakin University, 221 Burwood Hwy, Burwood, VIC 3125, Australia
renyue@deakin.edu.au

Abstract. In a wireless Federated Learning (FL) system, clients train their local models over local datasets on IoT devices. The derived local models are uploaded to the FL server which generates a global model, then broadcasts the model back to the clients for further training. Due to the heterogeneous feature of clients, client selection plays an important role in determining the overall training time. Traditionally, maximum number of clients are selected if they can derive and upload their local models before the deadline in each global iteration. However, selecting more clients not only increases the energy consumption of the clients, but also might not be necessary as having fewer clients in early global iterations and more clients in later iterations have been proved better for model accuracy. To address the issue, this paper proposes a client selection scheme which dynamically adjusts and optimizes the trade-off between maximizing the number of selected clients and minimizing the total communication cost between the clients and the server. By comparing the data diversity of clients, this scheme can select the most suitable clients for global convergence. A Diversity Scaling Node Selection framework (FedDS) is implemented to dynamically change the selecting weights of each node based on the degree of non-i.i.d data diversity. Results has shown that the proposed FedDS can speed up the FL convergence rate compared to FedAvg with random node selection.

Keywords: Federated Learning · Diversity Scaling · Convergence · client Selection

1 Introduction

Due to the increasing growth of processing capabilities at mobile edge nodes, networks are undergoing a paradigm shift from traditional cloud computing to a Mobile Edge Computing (MEC) system [1,2]. Federated learning (FL) is an emerging distributed machine learning (DML) technology that enables edge devices to jointly train a shared machine-learning model without the direct transmission of private data [3]. A fundamental challenge for FL is data heterogeneity. In contrast to previous optimisations in DML, where algorithms operate on independent and identically distributed (i.i.d.) data samples partitioned

© ICST Institute for Computer Sciences, Social Informatics and Telecommunications Engineering 2023
Published by Springer Nature Switzerland AG 2023. All Rights Reserved
W. Wang and J. Wu (Eds.): BROADNETS 2023, LNICST 511, pp. 126–137, 2023.
https://doi.org/10.1007/978-3-031-40467-2_8

from a huge dataset [4–6], in FL, models are trained on local clients by using local data, which are usually client-specific and have dissimilarities between each other. Furthermore, data samples on clients may not be independent and identical (non-I.I.D.). Thus, picking clients at random to take part in each training round can't show how the data is distributed globally. For example, under heterogeneous settings, random node selection has been proven to achieve extremely long training latency [4]. Training on clients with non-i.i.d. datasets will result in biased model updates, which will lower the overall convergence rate and accuracy of the model as well as necessitate additional rounds of communication for resource-constrained edge devices [5,6].

Due to the non-i.i.d Date issue, network uncertainty, bandwidth limitation, the straggler effect, etc. [7], participating clients (nodes) will have a substantial impact on the performance of FL. It is necessary to optimize the client selection procedure for performance purposes. In this paper, FedDS is a node selection strategy developed to increase the convergence rate of FL with non-iid nodes. By utilising a selection strategy based on selecting weights, it considers local nodes' diversity scaling to aggregate and determine the suitable subset of nodes for local training and global aggregation. Our main contributions are as follows:

– We propose FedDS, a node selection strategy that allows the server to dynamically adjust the selecting weights of each node in each round based on the diversity of participating nodes. FedDS favourably chooses the nodes that can help improve the model convergence.
– We evaluate how different local updates affect model training and suggest an aggregation algorithm that uses diversity scaling to evaluate how different the local nodes' updates are.
– We evaluate the performance of FedDS by conducting experiments on real datasets under varying heterogeneity settings. Results illustrate the efficacy of FedDS in accelerating the convergence rate of the FL model in comparison to the widely used FedAvg method [3].

2   Related Work

In general synchronous FL, nodes are randomly selected to participate in local training(e.g., FedAvg [3], FedProx [4],CMFL [8]). However, FL may have nodes with discrepancies in data quality and distribution, computational ability (e.g., CPU or GPU, memory size), network connectivity (e.g., traffic transmission speed), and constrained resources (e.g., limited bandwidth and energy budget). A well-designed node selection strategy is essential for FL performance enhancement. There are prior studies on node selection strategy, focusing on system heterogeneity and network connectivity [9,10]. For example, The authors in [9] presented a node selecting scheme by considering the resource conditions of nodes. Amiria et al. [10] introduced an algorithm to schedule nodes by calculating the $\ell2$-norm of local updates and transmission channel condition. The authors in [11] proposed a different strategy to achieve a faster convergence by choosing node with higher local loss. However, measuring the local loss of node in run time leads to additional communication and computation cost.

Several other works have focused on probabilistic-based node selection strategy, where every node has a chance of contributing to the global model. [12–16]. Particularly, Chen et al. [12] evaluated the contribution of each node based on the norm of local updates, hence calculating the chosen probability for each node. When bandwidth resources are restricted, nodes having a higher norm of local updates have a greater probability of getting selected, hence boosting the convergence rate. The authors in [13] utilised Artificial Neural Networks (ANNs) to estimate the model updates of nodes that are not given the bandwidth for transmission. After analysing the successfully transmitted updates, the additional received updates can further speed up the model convergence.

Ren et al. [14] presented a probabilistic selection strategy that takes into account the importance of local update and transmission latency. Chen et al. [15] proposed a sampling strategy which aims at selecting more important nodes. It used the local update norm to determine the chance of node being selected in the node sampling process, which in turn optimises the variance of local gradients for aggregation. Similarly, the authors in [16] utilised importance sampling method to choose nodes on the server side. Similar to [15], the node selecting strategy is to minimise the local gradient variance bound.

In contrast to previous studies, this paper analyses the effects of data heterogeneity, and proposes a scheme based on node selecting weights for participating node selection. It examines the diversity of local updates and their relationship with the global update before adjusting the selection weights of each node based on diversity scaling. Hence, when training on heterogeneous data samples across nodes, the diversity of local updates directly contributes to the upper bound of the global model change and, consequently, convergence rate, as demonstrated theoretically in Sect. 3.1.

The remaining sections are organised as follows. Section 3 provides the preliminary including the concept of Diversity Scaling and the challenge of non-i.i.d. data. In Sect. 4, the proposed aggregation algorithms and node selection scheme are discussed. Evaluation and results are discussed in Sect. 5, followed by the conclusion in Sect. 6.

3   Preliminaries

In this section, we first introduce the key concept (Diversity Scaling) used in our work, then discuss the challenge to FL on heterogeneous data.

3.1   Diversity Scaling

A general FL training round contains the following steps:

- Global model initialisation: The central server initialises a global model and broadcasts it to each node.

- Local node update: Each selected node performs local training using local data samples by mainly calculating its local updates based on the global model (e.g., stochastic gradient descent (SGD)).
- Global Model Aggregation: After local node finishes their local training, all participated nodes send their own updates to the central server for further aggregation. The central server aggregates these updates based on the predefined aggregation algorithm, then updates the former global model. In FedAvg [3], updates from participated nodes are averaged and added to the global model as defined in Eq. (1). The global model is updated at the end of round.

$$\Delta_{avg}^t = \frac{1}{K}(\Delta_1^t + \Delta_2^t + ... + \Delta_K^t)$$
$$w^{t+1} = w^t + \Delta_{avg}^t \tag{1}$$

- The above steps form one round of FL training. These steps are usually running several rounds until convergence is reached and/or a satisfactory global model accuracy is obtained.

After R rounds of training, the magnitude of weights w changing on the global model is shown in Eq. (2), t denote the tth training round.

$$\|w^R - w^0\| = \left\| \sum_{t=0}^{R-1} (w^{t+1} - w^t) \right\|$$
$$\leq \sum_{t=0}^{R-1} \|w^{t+1} - w^t\| = \sum_{t=0}^{R-1} \|\Delta_{avg}^t\| \tag{2}$$

From the above Equation, it can be seen that the upper bound weight changing on the global model is directly determined by the value of $\|\Delta_{avg}^t\|$, so as the convergence rate. Considering one extreme example, if all the participated nodes have the exact same updates, then it can be argued that there is no diversity in this given round of training. Therefore, the multitude of nodes can be replaced by a single node. Another extreme example is that if the updates of participated nodes can perfectly cancel each other after averaging, then $\|\Delta_{avg}^t\|$ will be 0. By analyzing these two extreme examples, it's more likely that nodes' updates won't be either perfectly coherent or decoherent. Instead, they'll be somewhere in between.

Diversity coefficient can be used to quantify the diversity in node updates and measures how different the updates to each node are, as shown in Eq. (3).

$$\gamma^t = \frac{\frac{1}{K}\sum_k \|\Delta_k^t\|}{\|\Delta_{avg}^t\|} \tag{3}$$

A larger value of γ means higher degree of dissimilarity between node updates. This is very likely when training on heterogeneous data samples. To tackle the data heterogeneity issue (non-i.i.d.) in FL, we propose FedDS, which is an modification to FedAvg. Our FedDS uses diversity scaling to account for the effect of node update diversity, as demonstrated in Section IV-A Aggregation Algorithm via Diversity Scaling.

3.2   Challenges to Non-i.i.d. Data Distribution

FedAvg can achieve an acceptable convergence rate by using random node selection strategy and a simple weight averaging design; however, when it comes to partial node selection and non-i.i.d. training data, the convergence rate is relatively slow [17], as also demonstrated in [5, 7, 11], and [18]. It has been proven that increasing the amount of local computing (i.e., more local updates) can reduce the number of communication rounds (a major bottleneck in FL [3, 7]) required for convergence. However, even with improved local computing [17, 19], unsatisfactory model performance on non-iid datasets still exist. This is due to the strong relationship between the data distribution and the local objective loss function.

Simple selection strategies such as the random selection result in data samples being distributed differently on the chosen nodes. Due to training instability, a FL model has trouble converging when dealing with a non-i.i.d. context because the model is more optimal to the local objective rather than the global objective.

From a data heterogeneity point of view, it is important to understand and analyse the non-trivial node selection strategies, finding and choosing the nodes that contribute more to model convergence. By quantifying the diversity in node updates and measuring how different the updates to each node are, nodes with updates that are adversely affect the global update could be identified. Further, by dynamically changing the selecting weights for those potential adverse local nodes, it can be expected that the nodes helping reduce global loss the most will have a better chance of being chosen in the next training round.

4   The Proposed Algorithms

To improve the convergence rate of federated learning, we design a node selection scheme by incorporating two algorithms. An aggregation algorithm (FedDS) takes node update dissimilarity into account via diversity scaling. It can identify those nodes with higher degree of dissimilarity to further reduce the expected decrement of global loss in each round. Then, based on the result of aggregation algorithm, a node selection algorithm is applied to dynamically adjust the selecting weights for each node to be selected for the next round. Consequently, the server can preferentially select nodes that propel a faster model convergence.

4.1   Aggregation Algorithm via Diversity Scaling

The proposed aggregation algorithm (FedDS) is an extension method to FedAvg. It takes γ into account via diversity scaling, as shown in Algorithm 1. A similar notion called gradient diversity can be found in [20]. It has been demonstrated that high similarity between concurrent gradient updates degrades the performance of mini-batch stochastic gradient descent algorithms. However, update diversity in this paper is distinct from the gradient diversity, and we employ it to speed up the federated training.

Note that when training for the first round, we still need to randomly select a subset of nodes S^t from all the nodes, denoted as K, since all the nodes by default have the same selecting weights. After each node performs local update, each node's update dissimilarity Δ_k^t is sent to the server for averaging and diversity coefficient γ calculation. Larger γ value indicates higher degree of dissimilarity between node updates in current round. For the purpose of speeding up the convergence rate, it can be observed that a lower diversity coefficient γ value (i.e., lower degree of dissimilarity between node updates) could lead to a faster model convergence. Hence, we choose the minimum value of γ. γ_{max} is adopted to keep the change of diversity coefficient in a certain range. In practise, setting γ_{max} to $\sqrt{K}$ works well. Since γ can be calculated directly from trainer updates after one round. Due to its specialty, γ can be then utilised in Algorithm 2 as a coefficient for updating the selecting weights of nodes.

In the following training rounds, the server needs to select a subset of nodes S^t based on the labeled selecting weights of each node, calculated by Algorithm 2 and denoted as P. Node with a higher P value, a node will have a higher chance of being selected for the next round.

4.2   Node Selection

To enhance the convergence rate of a global model, one can aim to preferentially select the nodes with a higher contribution when training the global model on a variety of nodes (e.g., nodes with i.i.d. dataset, as observed in [3,18]). As a result, we propose a node selection strategy that can dynamically modify the selecting weights for each node in each communication round. The node selecting weights can be reduced if their local updates share significant dissimilarity and slow model convergence. It is done based on their update diversity and data distribution heterogeneity, which can be distinguished by the output value γ of the proposed aggregation algorithm (FedDS). Specifically, according to Eq. (4), the selecting weights for nodes labelled by Algorithm 2 are decreased, while the selecting weights for all other nodes are increased.

$$\Delta p_i^t = p_i^t \times min[\beta^\gamma, 1], i \in S^t \tag{4}$$

where p_i^t denotes the selecting weights for node i in the t-th round, Δp_i^t denotes the selecting weights changing in the next round. min function returns the minimum value among two arguments. β value is adopted to keep the rate of selecting weights change in a stable range. Based on the experiment results, setting β to 0.7 is a good choice of balancing the tradeoff.

After getting the selecting weights change for the participating nodes in the current round and previous round, the selecting weights for the rest nodes also need be changed accordingly, as shown in Eq. (5)

$$p_i^{t+1} = \begin{cases} p_i^t - \Delta p_i^t & i \in S^t \\ p_i^t + \dfrac{\sum_{S^t} \Delta p_i^t}{|K - S^t|} & i \in K - S^t \end{cases} \tag{5}$$

Algorithm 1. Aggregation via Diversity Scaling

Input: P, S, K

1: Initialisation: global model w^0, accelerated global model $w^0_{acc} = w^0$.
2: **for** round $t \leftarrow 0, 1, 2, \dots$ **do**
3:     **Server**
4:     **if** $t == 0$ **then**
5:         Select S^t of K nodes based on P^0
6:         Send w^0 to nodes in S^t
7:     **else**
8:         Select a subset S^t with highest P of K nodes
9:         Send w^{t-1} to nodes in S^t
10:    **end if**
11:    **for each** node k *(in parallel)* in S^t **do**
12:        $w^t_k \leftarrow w^t_{acc}$
13:        $w^t_k \leftarrow w^t_k - \eta * \nabla f_k(w)$
14:        Send $\Delta^t_k = w^t_k - w^t_{acc}$ to server
15:    **end foreach**
16:    **Server**
17:    Update global model
18:        $w^{t+1} = w^t_{acc} + \Delta^t_{avg}$
19:    Update accelerated global mode
20:        $w^{t+1}_{acc} = w^t_{acc} + min(\gamma^t, \gamma_{max}) * \Delta^t_{avg}$
21:    Where
22:        $\Delta^t_{avg} = \frac{1}{K} \sum_k \Delta^t_k$ and $\gamma^t = \frac{\frac{1}{K} \sum_k \|\Delta^t_k\|}{\|\Delta^t_{avg}\|}$
23: **end for**
24: **return** $min(\gamma^t, \gamma_{max})$ for Algorithm 2

Algorithm 2. Node Selecting Weights

Input: $S, K, \gamma, \beta, p^t_i, i \leftarrow 1, 2, \dots, K$

1: Initialisation: $p^0_i = \frac{1}{K}$, w^0, $w^0_{acc} = w^0$
2: **for** round $t \leftarrow 1, 2, \dots$ **do**
3:     **Server**
4:         Sampling S^t nodes according to P^{t-1}_i
5:         $w^{t+1}, w^{t+1}_{acc}, \gamma \leftarrow$ ALGORITHM 1
6:         Updating the selecting weights $p^t_i, i \leftarrow 1, 2, \dots, K$, by (4), (5) for use in the next round
7: **end for**
8: **return** p^t_i for Algorithm 1

---

5   Evaluation and Analysis

We implement FedDS on different tasks with different hyper parameters and compare the results with FedAvg. Firstly, we demonstrated FedDS on speeding up the convergence rate of global model. Then, we tested FedDS under different level of data heterogeneity. We analyze the communication cost and complexity compared with FedAvg, as shown in Sect. 5.3. The adopted dataset, learning model and experiment settings are listed as follows:

In the experiments, we consider non-convex classification problem with MNIST [21] using a convolutional neural network (CNN) model. Specifically, this CNN model has 7 layers with two Convolutional layers $(5 \times 5 \times 10, 5 \times 5 \times 20)$, each of which is followed by 2×2 Max pooling. The second convolutional layer has 50% dropout, and two Fully Connected layers $(320 \times 50, 50 \times 10)$, followed by Softmax at the end. ReLu activation maps all of the Convolutional and Fully connected layers.

The initial learning rate, learning-rate decay, local batch size, and local epoch number are set to be 0.01, 0.995, 20 and 1, respectively. Although adjusting these parameters may improve the performance, it is out of scope of this paper, as we mainly focus on how to improve the training accuracy under non-i.i.d. dataset at client sites.

To implement different levels of data heterogeneity, we introduce two parameters μ and ν. Specifically, μ denotes the ratio of nodes which are equipped with i.i.d. dataset. ν denotes how many labels the nodes have. For example, if the number of total nodes $K = 50$, $\mu = 0.2$ means that $\mu K = 10$ nodes are i.i.d., $(1-\mu)K = 40$ nodes are equipped with non-i.i.d. dataset. $\nu = 3$ means that the data samples on these nodes evenly belong to 3 labels. As such, smaller μ and ν indicate a higher data heterogeneity.

5.1 Performance

We evaluate the test accuracy performance of the proposed FedDS by comparing with the baseline algorithm FedAvg. The level of data heterogeneity is $\mu = 0.5$, $\nu = 2$. In each training round, the server selects $S^t = 10$ nodes out of total 50 nodes randomly (selecting fraction $c = 0.2$) to join the training. For fair comparison, the selected nodes number in each round are the same for both FedDS and FedAvg.

As shown in Fig. 1, FedDS can achieve higher accuracy and lower training loss comparing to FedAvg. FedDS has faster convergence speed in several initial rounds due to the high diversity of local updates that caused by data heterogeneity. Thus for the next round training, reducing the selecting weights of those nodes whose local updates share significant dissimilarity is effective to speed up the model convergence.

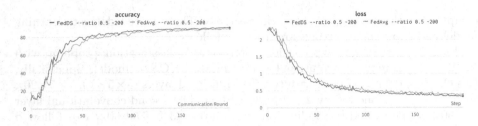

Fig. 1. Performance of the proposed FedDS vs FedAvg with –ratio(μ) = 0.5 - round ($T = 200$).

5.2   Data Heterogeneity

We evaluate the performance of the proposed algorithm in different data heterogeneity scenarios by using different fraction of non-i.i.d. nodes and labels for the participating nodes (i.e., $\mu = 0.3, 0.5, 0.7$ and $\nu = 1$).

As can be seen from Fig. 2, FedDS converges faster and achieves a higher test accuracy, compared with FedAvg regardless of different levels of data heterogeneity. Furthermore, as shown in Table 1, as the data becomes more heterogeneous, the performance improvement is greater (i.e., mu changes from 0.7 to 0.3).

FedDS performs better when the number of i.i.d. nodes is limited and the non-i.i.d. nodes have highly skewed data samples (e.g., $mu = 0.3, 0.5$), demonstrating FedDS's effectiveness in identifying nodes that have more contributions to the global model.

FedDS and FedAvg perform similarly in scenarios with the least amount of data heterogeneity (i.e., $mu = 0.7$). The reason is that non-i.i.d. nodes may not be selected to join the training when a large number of i.i.d. nodes are available.

5.3   Communication Cost

We evaluate the communication cost of the proposed algorithm and compare it with FedAvg. During the training process, a fraction of n nodes are selected to train a model whose size is N with T iterations to achieve a desired model. In each round, every node sends the local model with size of N to the server and receives the global model with size of N from the server, so the communication cost of each node is $2N \times T$. In general, training on the non-i.i.d data requires comparatively more training rounds to reach the convergence than the i.i.d data. Thus, a potential way to make comparison and to prove that the non-i.i.d data heterogeneity issue has been mitigated is to speed up the training convergence by reducing the communication round when setting a target accuracy. The comparison with FedAvg is shown in Table 2. It can be seen that our algorithm supports more efficient communications. The communication cost are reduced for all of the data heterogeneity settings to a target test accuracy (80%).

Table 1. Test accuracy comparison of FedDS and FedAvg with different settings of data heterogeneity.

Algorithm	$\mu = 0.3$	$\mu = 0.5$	$\mu = 0.7$
FedAvg	83.62%	88.52%	90.56%
FedDS	88.44%	90.79%	92.52%
Difference	4.82%	2.27%	1.96%

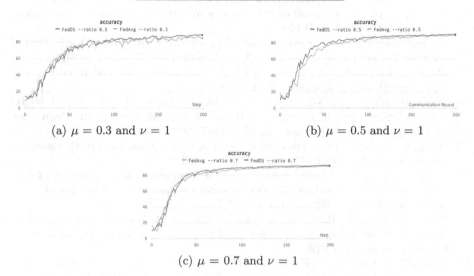

(a) $\mu = 0.3$ and $\nu = 1$ (b) $\mu = 0.5$ and $\nu = 1$

(c) $\mu = 0.7$ and $\nu = 1$

Fig. 2. Test accuracy over communication rounds of FedDS and FedAvg with different data heterogeneity settings.

Table 2. Communication round to achieve target test accuracy, comparison between FedDS and FedAvg with different settings of data heterogeneity.

Algorithm	$\mu = 0.3, \text{acc} = 80\%$	$\mu = 0.5, \text{acc} = 80\%$	$\mu = 0.7, \text{acc} = 80\%$
FedAvg	$T = 91$	$T = 82$	$T = 48$
FedDS	$T = 70$	$T = 48$	$T = 40$

6 Conclusion

In this paper, we have presented a node selection strategy, FedDS. It can select suitable nodes and speed up the convergence rate of model with non-i.i.d. datasets. FedDS can change the selecting weights of node in each training round dynamically based on the diversity of their data. It can sort out the suitable local updates from nodes by measuring the dissimilarity between node updates in the current round. The experimental results under different data heterogeneity settings have shown that FL training with the proposed FedDS can speed up the model convergence and gain higher test accuracy.

References

1. Chiang, M., Zhang, T.: Fog and IoT: an overview of research opportunities. IEEE Internet Things J. **3**, 854–864 (2016)
2. Xiong, Z., Zhang, Y., Niyato, D., Wang, P., Han, Z.: When mobile blockchain meets edge computing. IEEE Commun. Mag. **56**, 33–39 (2018)
3. McMahan, H.B., Moore, E., Ramage, D., Hampson, S., y Arcas, B.A.: Communication-efficient learning of deep networks from decentralized data. In: Proceedings of 20th International Conference on Artificial Intelligence and Statistics, pp. 1273–1282. PMLR (2017)
4. Li, T., Sahu, A.K., Zaheer, M., Sanjabi, M., Talwalkar, A., Smith, V.: Federated optimization in heterogeneous networks. arXiv:1812.06127 [cs, stat] (2020)
5. Zhao, Y., Li, M., Lai, L., Suda, N., Civin, D., Chandra, V.: Federated learning with non-IID data. arXiv:1806.00582 (2018)
6. Wang, H., Kaplan, Z., Niu, D., Li, B.: Optimizing federated learning on Non-IID data with reinforcement learning. In: IEEE INFOCOM 2020 - IEEE Conference on Computer Communications, pp. 1698–1707 (2020)
7. Wang, S., et al.: Adaptive federated learning in resource constrained edge computing systems. arXiv:1804.05271 [cs, math, stat] (2019)
8. Wang, L., Wang, W., Li, B.: CMFL: mitigating communication overhead for federated learning. In: 2019 IEEE 39th International Conference on Distributed Computing Systems (ICDCS), pp. 954–964 (2019)
9. Nishio, T., Yonetani, R.: Client selection for federated learning with heterogeneous resources in mobile edge. In: Proceedings of the IEEE International Conference on Communications (ICC) (2019)
10. Amiri, M.M., Gündüz, D., Kulkarni, S.R., Poor, H.V.: Convergence of update aware device scheduling for federated learning at the wireless edge. IEEE Trans. Wireless Commun. **20**, 3643–3658 (2021)
11. Cho, Y.J., Wang, J., Joshi, G.: Client selection in federated learning: convergence analysis and power-of-choice selection strategies. arXiv:2010.01243 (2020)
12. Chen, M., Shlezinger, N., Poor, H.V., Eldar, Y.C., Cui, S.: Communication-efficient federated learning. Proc. Natl. Acad. Sci. U. S. A. **118** (2021). https://doi.org/10.1073/pnas.2024789118
13. Chen, M., Poor, H.V., Saad, W., Cui, S.: Convergence time optimization for federated learning over wireless networks. IEEE Trans. Wireless Commun. **20**, 2457–2471 (2021)
14. Ren, J., He, Y., Wen, D., Yu, G., Huang, K., Guo, D.: Scheduling for cellular federated edge learning with importance and channel awareness. arXiv:2004.00490 (2020)
15. Chen, W., Horvath, S., Richtarik, P.: Optimal client sampling for federated learning. arXiv:2010.13723 (2020)
16. Rizk, E., Vlaski, S., Sayed, A.H.: Optimal importance sampling for federated learning. In: ICASSP 2021–2021 IEEE International Conference on Acoustics, Speech and Signal Processing (ICASSP), pp. 3095–3099 (2021)
17. Li, X., Huang, K., Yang, W., Wang, S., Zhang, Z.: On the convergence of FedAvg on non-IID data. In: Proceedings of the International Conference on Learning Representations (ICLR) (2020)
18. Wu, H., Wang, P.: Fast-convergent federated learning with adaptive weighting. IEEE Trans. Cogn. Commun. Netw. **7**, 1078–1088 (2021)

19. Stich, S.U.: Local SGD converges fast and communicates little. In: Proceedings of the International Conference on Learning Representations (ICLR) (2019)
20. Yin, D., Pananjady, A., Lam, M., Papailiopoulos, D., Ramchandran, K., Bartlett, P.: Gradient diversity: a key ingredient for scalable distributed learning. In: Storkey, A. and Perez-Cruz, F. (eds.) Proceedings of the Twenty-First International Conference on Artificial Intelligence and Statistics, pp. 1998–2007. PMLR (2018)
21. Lecun, Y., Bottou, L., Bengio, Y., Haffner, P.: Gradient-based learning applied to document recognition. Proc. IEEE **86**, 2278–2324 (1998)

A Modern Platform for Social Governance

Jinfeng Yu[1], Yuning Zhang[1], Wenda Teng[2], Yu Wang[2], Ning Hui[1],
and Delin Peng[2(✉)]

[1] National Engineering Laboratory of E-Government Modeling and Simulation,
Harbin Engineering University (HEU), 145 Nantong Street, Nangang District,
Harbin, China
yujinfeng@hrbeu.edu.cn

[2] Heilongjiang Provincial Committee of the Communist Party of China Political and
Legal Information Center, 45 Changjiang Road, Nangang District, Harbin, China
pdl1993@126.com

Abstract. With the rapid development of today's society, the traditional social and government management model has gradually emerged drawbacks, modern social management requires multi-sectoral integration of government resources to provide joint management and services. In addition, because the speed of economic development in the new era is far ahead of social management, the adjustment of the pattern of interests in social management and more weak links, resulting in conflicts and occasional incidents in the community increased, which requires social management work to reach a higher level. In recent years, China has actively explored and innovated in social governance and continuously improved the level of social governance. But the overall effect and management level still need to be further improved. This paper first expounds the basic connotation and category of social governance, and then comprehensively analyzes the problems existing in social governance. Combined with modeling and simulation system, intelligent governance support, GIS [9,10] and other technologies, after combing the business, the social comprehensive management information system is designed. The main application modules of the system include provincial and municipal standard platform module, provincial supervision module, data docking standard module, system docking module.

Keywords: MBSE · Social governance · Modern platform

1 Introduction

The most fundamental point of promoting the modernization of social governance is in the "social" field, and the core content of governance in the "social"

Supported by 2021 Heilongjiang Key Research and Development Plan. Research and Demonstration of Social Governance Integrated Platform Construction Heilongjiang Science and Technology Department Project Number: GA21C020.

field is to prevent, control and defuse conflicts and risks. In recent years, China has been attaching great importance to the development of social governance and actively promoting the construction of collaborative mechanisms. When dealing with social problems in provinces and cities themselves, there are many problems, such as difficulties in public reflection, difficulties in dealing with grassroots personnel, difficulties in supervising command centers, difficulties in coordinating units, and difficulties in commanding decision-making leaders [1–3]. These problems seriously affect the efficiency of social governance and seriously slow down the processing speed of social governance issues.

The "social governance modern management platform" project aims to solve the above problems by strengthening collaborative command, grassroots governance ability, and intelligent management platform, so that it can effectively break the information barriers between functional departments, integrate and share information resources, and improve the efficiency of comprehensive management [4,5].

2 Background

At present, social security governance in our country is in the process of transformation from a single subject to multiple subjects, and the cooperative governance mechanism among multiple subjects of social security governance needs to be rebuilt. The further development of social governance is affected by problems such as hidden dangers in function division, difficulties in collaborative command, immature social development, and inadequate system guarantee. These problems urgently need to be solved by modern information technology.

There are hidden dangers in the division of governance functions, and the powers and responsibilities of various departments are not clear enough. Since each governance body is independent, and there is no unified organization or department that can directly manage and directs all the governing bodies, in the actual process of governance, it is easy to appear problems such as overlapping responsibilities of various governance subjects, multiple management or mutual deniability, and lack of management, which lead to the unreasonable phenomenon of governance vacuum and reduced efficiency, affect the construction of collaborative governance mechanism, and affect the overall performance of social governance, to make it difficult to form governance synergy.

Insufficient data and information statistics lead to insufficient decision support. The information between various departments cannot be exchanged, the data is scattered and isolated, the existing precipitated data cannot be effectively utilized, and the information resources at the grassroots level cannot be timely collated and reported, which all lead to insufficient data support of personnel in social governance. The popularity of smart devices is not high, and there is a lack of corresponding early warning and prevention measures. Not yet able to achieve the liberation of manpower, comprehensive perception and the city is prone to a "problem blind Angle", and there is a lack of intelligent analysis models and algorithms adapted to application scenarios to support early warning and prevention.

The deployment and control ability of grid workers is weak, which cannot guarantee the working efficiency of grid workers. Most of the command and scheduling still stay in remote viewing and video consultation and do not play the real sense of command and scheduling [6, 7]. Finally, the single access channel of information is also a big problem. The current social governance information collection relies on the manual collection of grid workers and there is no corresponding more intelligent and automatic collection method, and the lack of channels for the masses to actively participate, which greatly limits the source and collection of governance information. At the same time, the intervention of social forces is also not formed, which has caused some obstacles to the construction of social co-governance forces and the formation of mass prevention and mass governance system.

3   Design Elaboration

In the design of this scheme, we fully consider meeting the new requirements of social governance development and construction [11], and at the same time consider the application of advanced technology to achieve social governance innovation [12–14]. Through the innovation of the social governance system and mechanism, we can accelerate the solution of the existing problems of relatively backward and inadequate social development, and realize the people's new demand for a better life. We will strengthen the development of coordination mechanisms, encourage the active cooperation and efforts of all types of cooperative governance entities, open up new prospects in social governance, and realize the modernization of social governance.

3.1   Building a Platform

With the goal of social governance construction, the platform is constructed to sort out and formulate unified standard and normative systems such as data standards, business standards, and interface standards and it collect the underlying general serviceability according to the standard specification, supporting the upper data, business, application and service of the upper layer, to ensure the smooth operation, efficient operation and continuous iterative upgrading of the platform. At the same time, the unified business assessment mechanism of the province is formulated, and according to the assessment mechanism, all cities (districts) and counties of the province are assessed to promote excellence.

The data on social governance in cities and regions of the province are gathered together. Through big data analysis, the in-depth mining and analysis of various thematic information are ensured to assist decision-making. The data on municipal social governance of the whole province will be collected and deeply mined. Through big data analysis and algorithm model matching, combined with the actual governance thematic scenes, the "municipal physical signs analysis report" supported by data is formed, and the municipal social governance provides the basis for decision-making. To build an integrated municipal social governance platform for the whole province, the provincial platform can coordinate the disposal across prefectures and cities, to achieve high-level coordination and overall planning.

3.2   Modeling Techniques

Advanced modeling and simulation technology (MBSE) [8] is adopted to conduct digital modeling of the social governance comprehensive platform construction model. It can quickly and efficiently build a model to simulate the real-world collaborative working process of government affairs, clearly show the process of government affairs processing subject, and deeply analyze the collaborative sharing needs of information systems.

The MBSE methodology is a collection of processes, methods, and tools that supports systems engineering disciplines in a "model-based" or "model-driven" context. Through a standard modeling language, construct system requirements model, function model, architecture model, implementation requirements, functional decomposition and distribution to the architecture, through the model execution, logic system requirements and functions of "verification" and "confirm" are achieved, and drive the joint simulation, product design, implementation, testing, integration, verification, and validation.

Model, transferred by MBSE, includes requirements, structure, behavior, and parameters of the dynamic information model, enables all kinds of professional engineering and technical personnel throughout the entire organization to understand and express the system more intuitively, to ensure that the whole process of transmission and use is based on the same model. Based on the goal-oriented business modeling method, this paper analyzes the operation mechanism of business data and information systems. The method of cross-department business collaboration and resource sharing is formed, and the solution to the problem of cross-department information sharing and business collaboration is developed from the aspects of the organization, application, and technology.

3.3   Modeling Techniques

It can achieve multi-level grid governance and fast dynamic information collection and help to realize the functions of cooperative command, research, and decision of social governance. The five-level grid governance system of province, city, district, county, town, and street, community (village) is constructed to realize the rapid and dynamic collection of various social governance elements and form an all-round, dynamic, and fine management and service pattern based on the grid unit. This function is expected to be provided by standard platform modules at the provincial and municipal levels.

It can realize the command and supervision of the whole process of the incident problem and can be coordinated and co-governed among different levels. Build the provincial supervision and coordination function module, establish a platform to construct multi-channel event acceptance methods, handle events according to the standard event processing process, realize unified supervision, ensure the operation of the process, and let the people participate in social governance, and gain a sense of participation, happiness and security.

For the public, one-click event submission is supported, and for the internal, a mobile terminal is established, so that events can be handled at any time. Through the construction of the management front desk, provide an effective external channel, so that the public can directly report information, and establish the corresponding information function, so that the public can directly communicate with the responsible department, and timely know the progress of incident processing. It also provides a safe and convenient mobile terminal inside the department, to manage the events in the grid uniformly.

The situation elements are presented and multidimensional decision analysis is carried out. It is necessary to comprehensively perceive the operational signs and social governance situation of the whole province. The dynamic information of social management should be studied and analyzed from multiple dimensions to assist leaders in making decisions and realizing the prediction and early warning of urban events in the province.

Department resources should be integrated to facilitate unified command and scheduling. Establish a unified system and standard to integrate and utilize data resources. Efforts are made to change the pain points of the past, which were governed by separate departments, and to gather information for the provincial command center, to realize the transformation from static control to dynamic control and from single management to comprehensive management.

AI technology is used to optimize service processes and develop intelligent business applications. Advanced technologies such as big data and artificial intelligence are used to achieve "intelligent acceptance, intelligent allocation, intelligent supervision, and intelligent return visits", comprehensively improve the efficiency of social governance and intelligent application, and realize the complementary of "grids on the ground and wisdom on the cloud".

3.4   Platform Architecture

The platform is mainly divided into three parts: governance center, governance application, and governance foreground. Among them, the governance platform is the bottom supporting part of the whole platform, which lays a solid foundation for the establishment and operation of the whole platform. Governance application is the main body of the whole platform, which is composed of four parts: provincial and municipal standard platform, provincial supervision and coordination, data docking standard, and system docking, which is the main function embodiment of the whole platform. The governance front desk is divided into two application ends, internal and external, respectively to undertake internal and external business management and other functions (Fig. 1).

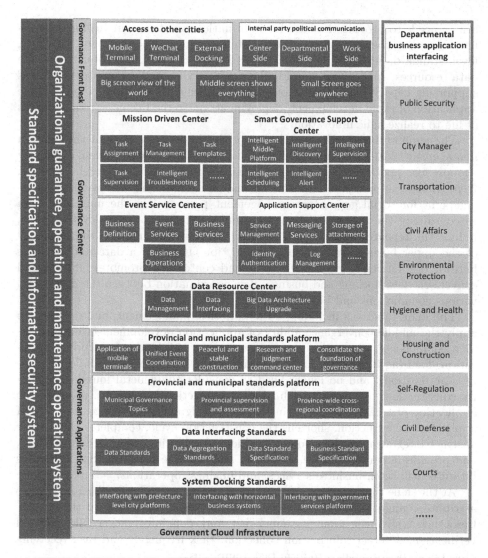

Fig. 1. Platform Architecture of Social Governance Modernization

4   Architecture Design

4.1   Govern the Middle Desk

The construction of the modern management platform of municipal governance cannot be separated from the foundation of the basic general capability, which is mainly the business general capability and the information general capability. To realize social governance at the municipal level, data and business need to be connected horizontally and vertically, social governance mechanisms and constitution need to be recursed from top to bottom, and solid support (framework) center needs to provide the base for information construction. Regional governance involves the data and business system, facing the source, type, quantity, level, standard, etc. a lot of "problems", requires the support center to provide data resources, application support, the event service, and driving tasks such as supporting capacity, to realize from different levels, up to support the flexible application of rapid development, deployment, make the business from all walks of life to realize agile innovation.

The support base is the foundation of the basic framework of the modern management platform of municipal governance and provides universal capability support for upper-level data turnover, business application, and service sharing. It provides a unified standard and normative system and management starting point for social governance management personnel in the municipal area to coordinate the standardization and implement the platform level by level, reduce the repeated construction, reduce the cost and increase the efficiency of the upper business application construction. It builds a data and business hub for the municipal governance command center and promotes efficient and convenient data docking and business flow coordination between the center and various commissions and bureaux.

The main functions including data statistics, management, and docking, to apply the middle convergence ability of application development-oriented common components, in a unified interface to support all kinds of the upper application, focusing its various functions only when it is applied in building business applications, and no longer need to consider the general foundation ability construction, to avoid the redundant construction investment, promote the application of a rapid change in innovation. It significantly reduces the cost of application construction, shortens the construction cycle, completes the further abstract integration of the common business capabilities of digital applications, and provides a comprehensive, real-time, and scalable platform that integrates business definition, business services, and business operations.

At the same time, the task configuration module provides flexible and diverse attribute configurations for different types of tasks. According to the regular tasks such as site inspection, personnel visit, and room information collection and verification, different information collection, task frequency and task receiving objects can be formulated to form task templates.

4.2   Governance Application

Governance application is divided into four modules: provincial and municipal standard platform, provincial supervision and coordination, data docking standard, and system docking.

Provincial and Municipal Standard Platform Module. The provincial and municipal standard platform module builds the provincial and municipal governance modernization platform, which mainly includes four modules: consolidating the governance foundation, unifying event coordination, research and command brain, and a mobile terminal application.

The provincial and municipal standard platform module builds the provincial and municipal governance modernization platform, which mainly includes four modules: consolidating the governance foundation, unifying event coordination, research and command brain, and a mobile terminal application.

The tamping governance module has the functions of intellectual governance support, map service, comprehensive governance foundation, knowledge base system, and so on. Wisdom for support is based on data gathered in the center of the data resource, adapts the processing large data architecture, combined with the artificial intelligence algorithm model, assigns energy to the upper business application, to realize found less blind area, comprehensive regulation, scheduling optimization recommendations, early warning and high automatic, classification, distribution boards, release the command center of human, avoid artificial defects.

Map service is the basic implementation of municipal social governance and the essential spatial geographic information system for the core business. It is necessary to superimpose functions and construct scenes on the GIS engine to better support the command center for municipal governance-related work.

The basic subsystem of comprehensive governance refers to the relevant standard documents of the national grid and comprehensive governance. The comprehensive information resources required by national standards and user requirements are unified, unified, and shared, and the basic comprehensive governance application is made by adapting the information. This System provides comprehensive governance information management tools for social governance-related users, meets the requirements of national policies and reduces costs, and increases efficiency. It makes the basic data clear at all levels for the municipal governance command center and provides basic capability support for the upper-level business, application, and decision-making of municipal governance.

The knowledge base system brings together the whole domain knowledge, and center management platform, and it can be finished through the base application report knowledge, knowledge audit, shelves, shelves, knowledge for knowledge, work order transfer knowledge, knowledge retrieval, knowledge view, and knowledge correction, reference, department, yellow pages, operational management, and knowledge service bulletins, etc., the public can complete knowledge evaluation and knowledge collection through basic applications.

Unify the event coordination subsystem, and manage events in the whole process and life cycle around governance events. Provide full-function and intelligent applications for business staff of social governance to bring better user experience; For the municipal governance command center, open up the cross-regional, cross-departmental and cross-platform event coordination process, track and handle governance events one by one, and promote the steady development of the modernization of social governance in the municipal area.

The research command brain has five modules: command scheduling, emergency response, decision research and judgment, risk prevention and control, and situational awareness.

The command and dispatch system needs to comprehensively integrate all kinds of social governance resources within the jurisdiction, and visually present them on GIS map to complete the construction of an urban resource cloud map in the province. In addition, various AI applications can be used to communicate with field staff on the urban resource cloud map, and direct remote command and scheduling can be carried out to achieve rapid coordination and efficient disposal of governance events.

The emergency disposal system supports incidents, the judgment of events, emergency plan, emergency disposal, report, and feedback, the emergency plan review scenarios, such as emergency events associated with the linkage department coordination, distribution of the situation, and disposal of feedback, check on the results, etc., realize the emergency disposal process of effective linkage between the various departments.

The decision research and evaluation system makes use of the municipal governance theme database formed by the aggregation and association of the data resource center, combined with intelligent algorithm analysis, and makes a large screen visual display according to the theme and the key index data of each theme.

The risk prevention and control system combines the huge and complex data gathered with artificial intelligence capabilities and algorithm models to form the intellectual governance support ability [15], which runs through the whole process of governance events in actual business scenarios, to realize the early warning and control of various hidden dangers and risks in the province.

A situational awareness system combined with the regional governance-focused application scenario, makes the data resource center of the standard library data and subject library data, according to the intelligent algorithm, do special visual display, let the command center can lead the whole situation of intuitive perception district social governance, from different levels and different dimensions grasp the overall situation of the province city run.

The mobile terminal provides two types of mobile application scenarios: staff end and public end, to meet the different needs of staff's daily work, public appeal reporting, information consultation, and so on.

The staff end is mainly equipped for grid workers and carries the reporting functions of community buildings, population collection applications, and various events. It will gradually cover all communities and all kinds of management services according to the actual situation. The other part is the department end, which provides mobile applications for handling events by functional departments so that the staff of functional departments can get rid of time and space restrictions, look at and treat events in real-time, deal with and give feedback in real-time, and improve the efficiency of event processing. At the same time, the central end is set up to provide mobile terminal office applications for the staff of the command center, so that the staff can get rid of the time and space restrictions, pay attention to the event demands from various channels and the disposal process of distributed events in real-time, and improve the overall efficiency of event circulation.

The business of the public end for the masses mainly has three modules: problem reporting, receiving feedback, and service evaluation. The people will give a brief description of the problems they find and then report them. Firstly, all the cases accepted are merged to form the case acceptance module, and then all the cases are assigned. Different cases are assigned to different departments for processing and carrying out case supervision at the same time. If the case does not pass the review or needs to be modified, it can be reassigned. People can receive news from the relevant departments on the official account and give certain feedback. The department manager accepts the command center administrator from the case and reviews the case, or decides the case back, in the process of disposal of the right time for pressing the case, then the command center administrator reviews the results of the case, and offline verification check, if the case is unqualified, back pay equal attention to, if qualified, the case will be closed and included in the statistics. People can also evaluate the service of the relevant departments of the government after the relevant problems are dealt with, and complain if they are not satisfied with the service process (Fig. 2).

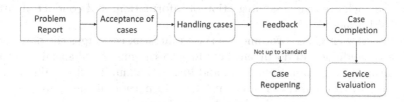

Fig. 2. Case processing flow chart.

Provincial Supervision Coordination Module. The provincial supervision and office coordination function module is constructed to facilitate the supervision, analysis, and coordination of social governance work in various cities, including supervision and assessment, data analysis, and cross-domain coordination. It mainly includes three parts: provincial supervision and assessment, municipal governance topics, and provincial cross-domain coordination.

The supervision and investigation part is mainly based on the needs of provincial departments, municipalities, and staff from different dimensions of assessment and statistics, and provides performance evaluation functions. It can quantitatively reflect the workload and work efficiency of provincial departments and social governance in various cities from multiple angles and dimensions according to the performance assessment rules and provides ability support for the realization of data-oriented and intelligent assessment.

The special topic of municipal governance shows the running situation of a map of social governance of the whole province from three aspects: urban management situation, market supervision situation, and comprehensive governance situation. From the perspective of business analysis of social governance, enhancing the capability and level of social governance as the goal, according to the "user-centric" principle, with the whole life cycle of the operation objects as the breakthrough point, concerns for the convenient degree, etc., at the same time around with the focus of social governance and innovation characteristics, grasp key, find brand and characteristic. To continuously help the government to timely find the problems in social governance business, and promote the closed-loop management mode of the whole process of social governance.

System Docking Module. Connect with existing municipal governance platforms in various cities, break the barrier of the provinces and cities system data and work order, unify construction of the province's event linkage docking module, establish unified standards and specifications for business connection, need docking information including business gathering information and delivery business cooperation at the provincial level and other systems to submit the business information together.

The provincial municipal governance platform should connect with the horizontal business system at the same level, break through the barriers of data circulation, achieve seamless integration of information, and conduct all-around linkage of business.

It connects with the government service platform, converges the data such as certificate handling and document handling to the municipal social governance data sharing and exchange platform, and forms the municipal social governance data standard through the cleaning and transformation of the aggregated data, which can be shared and called by other platforms.

Data Docking Standard Module. The provincial data docking standards and specifications have been formulated, and the municipal platform has been connected to the provincial platform according to the standards to realize the data sharing and exchange of the whole province. Meanwhile, the horizontal department systems related to political and legal business (including public security and government services) are also connected according to the corresponding data standards.

First, establish a unified standard for data [16]. The platform provides data verification and transaction processing mechanisms to ensure the integrity of data. The data should follow a unified specification, and uniform coding and the data set is maintained in a unified format. The consistency of the same index in different applications in the system should be ensured. The consistency of the same index data in different dimensions and granularity should be ensured. The recorded information must be accurate and cannot contain exceptions or errors. At the same time, the platform should be able to complete the collection and exchange of data triggered by all departments in real-time in the case of good network conditions.

After that, the data access standards of various government information systems will be established, including databases, files, messages, service interfaces, etc. The database access mode adopts the form of a front exchange information base and the data sharing exchange platform to connect. In this mode, the information exchanged between the department's government affairs application system and other departments application systems is transferred through the department's front exchange information base. The file access mode adopts the file exchange mode to exchange data with the data-sharing exchange platform. In this mode, the department saves the relevant data into XML and Excel files (Xls, Xlsx, or CSV format), and then sends the files to the municipal data sharing and exchanging platform through FTP, HTTP, etc., or obtains exchange information from the municipal data sharing and exchange platform. The message access mode connects the department to the data-sharing exchange platform in the form of a message service interface. In this mode, the department application system directly sends the exchange information to the data-sharing exchange platform by calling the message service interface or obtains the exchange information from the data-sharing exchange platform, without reading and writing the database. In the service interface access mode, the RESTfulAPI or Web-Services provided by the department are quickly connected to the data-sharing exchange platform and the service bus provides services for external applications. In this mode, the department needs to provide an explicit RESTfulAPI or WebService invocation interface.

The business standard specification is shown in the following table (Table 1).

Table 1. The business standard specification.

Number	Standard Name	Introduction
1	Social governance assessment and evaluation criteria	Establish a set of scientific and perfect assessment standards for provincial departments, cities, and staff in social governance
2	Event coding specification	Formulate coding rules and norms around the coding of municipal social governance event catalog, event list, and work order
3	Event List Directory	Form an event list according to the field, category, and directory around the social governance events in the municipal area

The data standard specification is shown in the following table (Table 2).

Table 2. The data standard specification.

Number	Standard Name	Introduction
1	Encoding specification for social governance data resources	Standardize data integration access and update strategies for social governance projects, customize update interfaces for various types of data, standardized data collection methods, and stipulate quality inspection methods
2	Social governance data integration access specification	Standardize the data elements of the basic information resource database of urban parts database and housing database
3	Data element specification of social governance infrastructure	Standardize the data elements of the basic information resource database of urban parts database and housing database
4	Social governance data governance specifications	Mainly include the requirements of data extraction, data cleaning, data conversion, and data loading
5	Social governance data quality specification	Determine data quality indicators and verify and monitor data quality problems; the basic technical requirements such as the technical methods of data quality inspection, data verification rules, data quality indicators, and data quality evaluation are stipulated
6	Social Governance database design specification	The name, table structure, metadata, characters, views, SQL encoding and applicable objects of the application database designed for each business topic of the social governance project will be standardized to ensure that each database can achieve unified and complete support for the application requirements of all data resources
7	Video front-end point basic information data specification	The basic information specification of front-end point location includes location information, jurisdiction information, time information, and camera information. Image information annotation area setting; Camera latitude and longitude and camera national standard coding code

5   Conclusion

Based on the comprehensive analysis of the current problems in social governance, this paper puts forward the coping strategies of unifying standards, establishing application channels, improving technical support, national governance, and intelligent support, which has reference significance for further improving the comprehensive governance ability of society. At the same time, it makes use of a modeling and simulation system (MBSE), puts forward the main construction contents of the platform, system construction model based on the current mainstream to detailed analysis and design of the system, adopts the design idea of platform and modularization, based on the unified complete system of technical standards and specifications, designs the social comprehensive governance management system which has been a realization, realizes real-time collection, transmission, storage and management, land, material, situation, matter, organization information, and designs and implements the collaborative workflow and evaluation mechanism.

Through the construction and application of the social comprehensive management system, this paper solves the following problems in the current social comprehensive management work: (1) Improve the communication between stakeholders of comprehensive social governance, and help the modelers to understand the complex structure of comprehensive social governance. (2) By enabling the system model to observe the social comprehensive governance business from multiple aspects and providing the ability to analyze the impact of social comprehensive governance business change, the complex social comprehensive governance business model will be constructed. (3) To improve the analysis quality of complex structures of integrated social governance by providing an unambiguous and accurate system model of integrated social governance that can assess consistency, correctness, and completeness. (4) Enhance knowledge capture and information reuse by capturing information in a more standardized way and making efficient use of the built-in abstraction mechanism inherent in model-driven methods. It is helpful to standardize and optimize the comprehensive social governance process and improve work efficiency. (5) Improve the ability to analyze and understand the business of comprehensive social governance by providing clear and unambiguous concept expression. Once you have learned MBSE, you will have mastered the method of constructing the complex structure of comprehensive social governance efficiently and standardly.

In the future, we will make MBSE modeling technology combined with social comprehensive treatment more closely, and more in-depth research, striving to provide more powerful support for comprehensive social governance through modeling and simulation technology.

References

1. Jun, L., Zhenyong, G.: Analysis and construction of the "three-pillar" model of urban social. J. Open Univ. GuangDong **030**(005), 99–105 (2021)
2. Nansheng, M.: Economic value analysis of comprehensive management of social security. Mark. Manag. Rev. (1), 3 (2022)
3. Laiming, Z., Lihui, L.: Theory and practice of social governance in New China. J. Manag. World **38**(1), 20–34 (2022)
4. Zengxiang, L., Jiandong, S., Wenyuan, L.: Improving social comprehensive management ability based on public security video surveillance network project. Commun. Manag. Technol. (004) (2021)
5. Jin, L.: Research on improving comprehensive management ability of network society in new period. Netinfo Secur. (S01), 4 (2020)
6. Shuangxi, Z.: Grid innovation of social governance. People's Tribune (2015)
7. Yonghe, Y.: Grid governance: informatization path and practice of promoting diversified resolution of disputes. Ind. Sci. Tribune **21**(5), 205–206 (2022)

8. Mann, C.: A practical guide to SysML: the systems modeling language. Kybernetes **38**(1/2), 989–994 (2009)
9. Xilei, Z.: Construction and application of social management system based on CIS. Ph.D. dissertation, Shandong University (2018)
10. Xinyuan, C., Zhao, L., Libo, G., Yinchao, L.: The management and application of gridding plus based on GIS: a case study of Pingfang District in Harbin City. Bull. Surveying Mapp. (S02) (2021)
11. Huiying, A., Chaofeng, H.: Research on the holistic governance of China's grassroots society in the post-epidemic era. J. Soc. Sci. (8), 8 (2021)
12. Chen, Z., Huang, H., Xu, Y., Xu, J.: Construction of comprehensive management information platform based on 'Xueliang project'. (6), 2 (2019)
13. Zhixu, H.: The design and implementation of information system platform for social management and comprehensive improvement. Ph.D. dissertation, Shandong University
14. Tianlei, Z.: The design and implementation of social comprehensive management information system. Ph.D. dissertation, Harbin Institute of Technology (2018)
15. Junjie, J.: Holistic smart governance: goal choice and system construction of China's megacities governance. Theory Reform (3), 11 (2022)
16. Zhongqiang, L., Shuai, H., Liqiang, X.: Interpretation and application of basic data specification for comprehensive management of social security. China Standardization (15), 63–65, 78 (2021)

Author Index

© ICST Institute for Computer Sciences, Social Informatics and Telecommunications Engineering 2023
Published by Springer Nature Switzerland AG 2023. All Rights Reserved
W. Wang and J. Wu (Eds.): BROADNETS 2023, LNICST 511, p. 153, 2023.
https://doi.org/10.1007/978-3-031-40467-2

Printed in the United States
by Baker & Taylor Publisher Services